BRITISH POLITICS AND THE AMERICAN REVOLUTION

British History in Perspective

General Editor: Jeremy Black

PUBLISHED TITLES

C. J. Bartlett *British Foreign Policy in the Twentieth Century*
Jeremy Black *Robert Walpole and the Nature of Politics in Early Eighteenth-Century Britain*
D. G. Boyce *The Irish Question and British Politics, 1868–1986*
John W. Derry *Politics in the Age of Fox, Pitt and Liverpool*
Ronald Hutton *The British Republic 1629–1660*
Diarmaid MacCulloch *The Later Reformation in England, 1547–1603*
Keith Perry *British Politics and the American Revolution*
A. J. Pollard *The Wars of the Roses*
Michael Prestwich *English Politics in the Thirteenth Century*
Robert Stewart *Party and Politics, 1830–1852*

FORTHCOMING TITLES

John Davis *British Politics, 1885–1931*
Ann Hughes *Causes of the English Civil War*

`1901165337`

Series Standing Order

If you would like to receive future titles in this series as they are published, you can make use of our standing order facility. To place a standing order please contact your bookseller or, in case of difficulty, write to us at the address below with your name and address and the name of the series. Please state with which title you wish to begin your standing order. (If you live outside the UK we may not have the rights for your area, in which case we will forward your order to the publisher concerned.)

Standing Order Service, Macmillan Distribution Ltd,
Houndmills, Basingstoke, Hampshire, RG21 2XS, England.

British Politics and the American Revolution

Keith Perry

M MACMILLAN

First published 1990

Published by
MACMILLAN EDUCATION LTD
Houndmills, Basingstoke, Hampshire RG21 2XS
and London
Companies and representatives
throughout the world

Filmset by Wearside Tradespools
Fulwell, Sunderland

Printed in Hong Kong

British Library Cataloguing in Publication Data
Perry, Keith
British politics and the American Revolution—(British
history in perspective ISSN: 0955–8322).
1. North America. British colonies. Colonies
administration. Resistance by colonies, history
I. Title II. Series
322.4'2
ISBN 0–333–40461–0 (hardcover)
ISBN 0–333–40462–9 (paperback)

CONTENTS

Contents

To Hugh and Judith

INTRODUCTION

How could a country, proud of its reputation as the home of 'free-born Englishmen' and reared on the idea of the necessity of Empire for continued security and national greatness, lose so significant a portion of her colonies so quickly? And how could the American colonists who had helped defend the Empire and were so proud of their Britishness so quickly be driven to leave it?

The temptation is to juxtapose the liberty-loving Americans defending freedom and parliamentary democracy with the foolishness, ignorance and corruption of British politicians and the tyranny and madness of George III. Such temptation has not always been resisted in the past, and its residue is still to be found in text books. But we have long since ceased to see George III as fool, tyrant and madman, and politicians are coming to be understood as men of their time, grappling with severe problems and doing so with as much honesty, self-seeking and hard work as any other politicians in any other age, according to the ideas and presuppositions of their time and order within the limits of practical politics. They were handicapped by a failure of language and understanding. When words like sovereignty and representation mean different things to men for whom law is the language and defence of political beliefs it can lead to bitter conflicts of principle.

We have come to appreciate from the work of Pole, Maier and Gipson that America was no democracy either in 1763 or in 1776.[1] Few colonies had a truly democratic franchise before the advent of President Jackson. Property qualifications were necessary for participation in the election of legislators and religious disabilities applied in most colonies. All colonies were run by oligarchies, 'gentrified' as in Virginia; or mercantile as in Massachusetts and Pennsylvania, while settlers on the frontiers of many colonies were grossly under-represented, though taxed. For much of our period only the eastern seaboard towns of America, dominated by such cities as New York, Boston and Charleston, were seriously involved in active opposition to British policy, while during the War of Independence many frontiersmen took up arms for King George against their eastern persecutors. 100 000 Loyalists left America after the defeat of Britain and many more Americans were unhappy at the turn of events. The population of Boston in 1763 was less than 20 000; that of the colonies less than two million. Thus the war in the colonies was a civil war too. Pauline Maier has shown the way in which a small group of radicals, aided by popular élitist reactions to British policy, were able to turn loyal colonists into, often nervous, supporters of independence.[2]

The story of American actions and reactions has been told very well elsewhere. This book is concerned only with the way British politics affected, and was influenced by, what happened in America. There are no heroes or anti-heroes in this story. No one individual can be blamed for the loss of the colonies. The degree of unanimity among the British ruling élite is the most obvious fact to emerge from a story of these events, and although some historians might wish that 'popular politics' would show considerable support for the colonists' cause, the evidence for any such sympathy is as patchy as is the evidence for any widespread dissatisfaction with the social and political order itself.

Benjamin Franklin was not the only contemporary to note that hostility to American pretensions was a failing not only of the administration of the time but of the British people.[3]

Politicians of any age may be foolish, venal, and even wicked but those of the eighteenth century were no worse, and in many cases, were a great deal better than those of other centuries, and it would be naive to argue that a whole political class, or a whole nation, could be characterised by a desire to tyrannise, or by foolishness. The politicians of any century are products of their time, share assumptions and act within the bounds of their own perceptions of things. Those of George III's reign held views about Empire and its crucial importance to Britain's survival as a power inevitable in men of their generation and breeding. With the possible exception of Pitt they were convinced of the virtues of a system based on the sovereignty of Parliament, a Parliament balancing the elements of monarchy, aristocracy and 'democracy' in such a way as to preserve liberty with order. True, none had first-hand knowledge of the colonies, but then the same could have been said of those later ministers who presided over the acquisition and relinquishment of the second British Empire. If all ministers were required to be intimately informed of their areas of responsibility few would ever be chosen; then as now they relied on the opinions and expertise of advisers who were generally of high quality. The ministers were conservative men of aristocratic origin whose fears of prerogative and belief in the virtues of parliamentary sovereignty made them act as they did towards American pretensions. They were not hostile to individual liberties, as reluctance to resort to arms amply proves. So it is to the way that politicians perceived the colonial system that we must look for the origins of British policies and reactions to the deeds of Americans.

Nor should we look to George III as originator of any tyranny in the colonies. George was neither mad nor bad and few monarchs can have had a deeper attachment to the constitution which it was his pride and duty to defend. Indeed the King's failing was rather to be too rigid in its defence. He was never responsible for making policy for America and rarely attempted to influence the responsible politicians to change their designs. Only three times in this period did the King seek to influence a House of Commons vote and on one of these occasions it was at the request of the ministry itself.

But George shared the prejudices and preconceptions of his ministers in full measure. The Declaratory Act summed up his views on the relationship of the colonies to Parliament fully and in the prolonged crisis George saw himself as defender of the rights of Parliament though not in any vindictive way, as his advice on the Mutiny Bill of 1766 and his preference for modification, rather than repeal, of the Stamp Act demonstrate. The King refused the opportunity to increase his influence and power implicit in the idea that he was King of Massachusetts equally as he was King of Great Britain. Puzzled, offended and finally insulted by what he saw as colonial disloyalty and rebellion, only at the last did the King insist on a military solution.

1
ORIGINS AND PURPOSES

The Structure of Colonial Government

Thirteen colonies were to declare their independence of the British Parliament and Crown in 1776. In general these were the colonies with the largest and most prosperous populations of white settlers: Massachusetts, New Hampshire, Rhode Island, Connecticut, New York, New Jersey, Pennsylvania, Maryland with its satellite colony of Delaware, Virginia, the two Carolinas and Georgia. In Newfoundland, Nova Scotia and the eight Caribbean colonies there was no rebellion despite a similar constitutional relationship to King and Parliament.

In a sense all thirteen colonies were Crown colonies since the constitutions of all were the consequence of acts by the Crown, but these colonies were of three types. Two colonies, Rhode Island and Connecticut, were charter colonies, established in the seventeenth century in the form of chartered companies. In these the Governor, Lieutenant-Governor, many officials and the Governor's council were annually and popularly elected, and in Rhode Island the assembly – as in Connecticut popularly elected – chose most of the minor officials each year. The charter colonies were the most independent of London's rule, partly because of the degree of popular control over the executive and partly because of

1

the eighteenth century's extreme reluctance to interfere with chartered rights or liberties secured by long usage.

There were three proprietary colonies, Pennsylvania, Maryland and Delaware, which by 1763 shared its Governor with Maryland. In such colonies the form of government depended on the charter granted initially to the Governor by the King, who took care to reserve rights to the Crown, and on the privilege granted by the owner to his settlers. Thus the three colonies displayed some variety of practice. Pennsylvania, unlike the other twelve colonies, had a unicameral legislature, the Governor's council being purely advisory. In all these colonies the Governor, chosen by the proprietor's interest with Crown approval, usually on instruction, could refuse legislation, which was also subject to privy council veto.

The remaining examples were Crown colonies operating under more or less identical constitutions, except for Massachusetts which enjoyed special privileges and protection, through the charter granted by William and Mary in 1691. These constitutions were based on the commissions issued by the Crown to the Governor, the King's representative and deputy, at the time of his appointment. In this sense the Crown's control was absolute, since no royal authority existed without the commission, and the commission with its instructions to the appointed Governor was in a sense a constitution. In practice no attempt was made before 1774 to alter the established system of representative institutions consisting of an elected assembly and a Governor's council chosen by the Governor, or by the assembly subject to the Governor's veto. However there was a potential source of conflict between colonists who became used to seeing their assemblies as permanent and equal, within the colonies, with Parliament, and a colonial system which still saw them as distinctly subordinate institutions with no authority other than that derived from the Crown. This confusion marked the imperial system as it developed in the eighteenth century, and the development of English constitutional ideas and practice towards the concept of parliamentary sovereignty, a notion foreign to the seventeenth century when the majority of the colonies were founded, piled confusion on confusion.

In theory at least most of the colonies enjoyed, or endured, a status of subordination to the authorities in London. In addition to the Westminster Parliament's powers over the colonies, the limits of which were disputed and disputable, the Crown exercised influence through the privy council's right to veto the legislation of colonial assemblies, its role as the venue for petitions and appeals from colonial courts and its preparation of commissions and instructions for Governors and other colonial officials. In effect its role was to preserve the prerogatives of the Crown in the colonies, acting on the advice of the responsible ministers of those departments with a role in colonial administration.

The Governor had substantial authority. Appointed by the King and ministers, enjoying the power to choose many of the officials in the province, he was in charge of executing the legislation of Parliament and the assembly in the colony and he was virtual Commander-in-Chief. Although in most cases required to act with the advice of his council that body was largely chosen by himself. The Governor could adjourn, prorogue or dissolve the assembly, and only in Massachusetts, South Carolina and New Hampshire were regular and frequent elections required by law. He was also obliged to refuse loyal assent to laws passed by the assemblies which conflicted with the laws of Great Britain.

One of the weaknesses of British control lay in the fragmented nature of administrative supervision. The Board of Trade, with its superior knowledge of colonial affairs, acted as a clearing station and storehouse of information and the chief advisory body to the privy council, but failed to achieve the leading executive role in colonial affairs, even under the vigorous leadership of the Earl of Halifax. The Secretary of State for the South also had responsibilities, and frequently clashed with the Board of Trade, while in wartime the Secretary at War would also be involved. The Admiralty and the Board of Customs would both have responsibility for proper obedience to the laws of trade. Other departments might also be involved, but few could withstand the growing authority over all the administration of the First Lord of the Treasury, whose office began to have directing influence on colonial policy and who as leader of the effective cabinet could oversee policies in other departments.

Studies of British colonial administration in the century preceding the Stamp Act by James Henretta[1] and Dora Mae Clark[2] agree closely in their conclusions. They show that the Treasury came to exert paramount influence over colonial policy and that Parliament was increasingly obliged to augment its responsibility for the expenses of the colonies while at the same time Treasury policy enabled colonial assemblies to achieve a considerable degree of independence.

In the early part of the century it was the Treasury's insistence that the colonies should be self-sufficient which prevented any subordination of colonies to Crown. Governor Shute, who was in the 1720s in dispute with the Massachusetts assembly, sought to revise the charter in order to provide the Governor with a fixed, permanent salary. When the Board of Trade urged that until the representative should be in a better temper Shute should be paid from the Exchequer, Sir Robert Walpole, First Lord of the Treasury 1721–1742, refused on the grounds that each colony should be self-supporting. The Board's subordination to the Treasury is obvious and not even the Earl of Halifax's vigorous presidency (1742–1754) altered this situation. The Duke of Newcastle, at the time of the incident Secretary of State for the South, understood the issue: 'what was lately practised by the House of Representatives in New England had [tended] to encroach upon His Majesty's prerogative'.[3] But he gave the Board no positive support and it is difficult to know how assemblies could have been coerced. Deputy-Governor Spotswood of Virginia on a later occasion wrote '... if the Assembly ... would stand Bluff he did not see how they could be forced to raise money against their will, for if they should direct it to be done by Act of Parliament ... (though it be against the Right of Englishmen to be taxt but by their

4

Representatives) yet they wou'd find it no easy matter to put such an act in execution.'[4]

.. It suited Walpole and his successors to let sleeping dogs lie; there was, as we have already seen, a feeling of unease about coercing an assembly, particularly one with rights defined by charter, and as Governor Colden of New York noted: 'they will be backward in espousing anything that looks like forcing in the giving of Money'.[5] Practical and philosophical objections to force were emphasised by the belief of the Treasury that the colonies should be self-sufficient.

The political consequences of these policies – or lack of them – were not that the colonies did become financially more self-sufficient but that administration and defence became an increasing burden on London, because the question of colonial contributions to the Empire was always kept at bay. In America the consequences of Treasury dominance were equally serious. The Governors, the King's representatives, became financially dependent on the assemblies, weakening control from London and emphasising the assemblies' equality with Parliament. The Massachusetts House of Representatives in 1732 remonstrated that 'the Taxing of the People, and Putting Money in the Treasury, is what more peculiarly belongs to the House of Representatives, as their constituents pay for it'.[6]

Treasury influence did not end there. The chief concern of Walpole, Pelham and Newcastle was always to secure their domestic political base and one means of doing so was to use colonial patronage. All departments with a colonial role had some patronage at their disposal; according to Henretta, Newcastle had 40 such gifts to bestow in 1730.

But the Treasury successfully fought to keep the lion's share of colonial patronage from Governorships and Deputy-Governorships to minor offices. The impact on the effectiveness of royal administration can be seen from the fact that many offices were held by colonists deputising for the English holder. But in addition, control from London seriously curtailed what little patronage the Governors had, made office holders look to London rather than to provincial capitals and left local patronage firmly in assembly hands. 'No wonder if a Governor be not clothed with Authority when he is stripped naked of power', wrote the Governor of South Carolina in 1748.[7] To this situation we need to add the development of private networks of patronage by politicians like Newcastle, and by minor officials in departments building up personal followings in America. It becomes clear that a coherent policy in America particularly to assert Crown or parliamentary control, involving conflict, was not likely to emerge in the circumstance of the reigns of George I and George II.

But the dire consequences of this situation can be exaggerated. Although Treasury influence in British politics and the tendency to avoid controversy did create problems for the future they did so only in the context of a new situation created by war and the counting house mind of George Grenville who had become First Lord of the Treasury in 1763 on Bute's resignation. The Treasury control in the reigns of George I and George II, fortified by the aristocratic Whiggism of the Old Corps of Whigs which dominated governments in the reigns of the first two Georges, might have helped to diminish the influence of the governors in the colonies and increase the self-esteem of the assemblies, but it also did nothing to challenge the control of the assemblies by an American oligarchy, gave little ammunition to radical opponents of Governor and élites and avoided serious constitutional conflicts with Westminster. The words of Governors Spottswood and Colden suggest that constitutional conflict between colonial assemblies and Westminster could have occurred with great ill temper well before George III's reign if matters had been pursued as the Board of Trade and its allies had wished. French hostility was a major reason why both sides would wish to avoid serious disputes but so also was the common interest of Governors and oligarchies in maintaining their own social, economic, and political hegemony. John Adams' appalled response to James Otis's 1761 doctrine that 'every man was an independent sovereign subject to no law, but the law written on his heart'[8] shows how far the wealthy ruling group of New England was from showing radical pretensions.

Moreover the administration in Britain, though it impinged on America at several points, did so in most cases with a light touch and with little or no co-ordination. The Atlantic also provided a barrier to effective control and few politicians of the first rank had real personal knowledge of the colonies. This does not imply ignorance. Lord Halifax when he was President of the Board of Trade and Plantations acquired an expertise unrivalled by any of his colleagues, largely from the permanent officials of his department, and Charles Townshend, one of his successors, also acquired firm opinions about the need for reform from the same sources. Benjamin Franklin referred particularly to the Permanent Secretary of the Board of Trade, John Pownall brother of Thomas, MP for Tregony and former Governor of Massachusetts, and deemed him to 'have a strong bias against us and to infect them [the Presidents] one after another as they come to it'.[9] Equally, long service in the Board of Trade gave men like Soame Jenyns (1755–80), Edward Eliot (1759–76) and George Rice (1761–70) real expertise and influence. Therefore it is not true to say, as did Chief Justice William Allen of Pennsylvania, that ministers were 'deficient ... in the knowledge of American affairs'.[10] But the Board of Trade failed in the eighteenth century to win for itself the dominant executive role in colonial affairs. Only with a sympathetic First Lord and a postwar financial crisis would their ideas win a hearing where it really counted. At least until the reign of George III the Treasury was largely instrumental in avoiding constitutional crisis in relations with the colonies. Until 1763, the two most obvious ways in which the colonies were subject to control from Britain were by the ultimate reliance on Britain for protection from the might of France and Spain and by the fact that, as colonies, they existed for the economic benefit of the mother country. This economic dependence, under which the colonists occasionally chafed, but from which they also undoubtedly benefited, was among the chief reasons for British politicians' unanimous determination to keep the Empire intact. British commercial prosperity, sea power and security from the Catholic powers were seen to be bound up with that Empire.

The Navigation and Trade Acts from 1659 onwards, barring foreign ships from colonial ports and giving British and colonial shipping a monopoly of the imperial carrying trade, were the cornerstone of this system. They protected sea power, gave Britain first call on raw materials from the colonies and helped build the profits of British sea ports and merchants. A growing list of colonial items, the enumerated articles, could be exported only to Britain, but many more of the colonists could sell where they wished. British control was not by any means a great disadvantage to the colonists. After 1783 the patterns of American trade did not appreciably alter and Jefferson, when President of the United States 1801–9, recognised that America was still of necessity tied to 'the apron strings of the Royal Navy'. The Molasses Act demonstrates how carefully the Empire sought to balance competing interests, in this case of the British West Indies and New England, but it still existed to serve British interests first and foremost. Various statutes, the Wool, Hat and Iron Acts for example, were designed to protect home industries from colonial competition while shortage of specie in the colonies, especially Virginia, resulted from protection of British creditors.

Although colonists benefited from being part of the Empire and enjoyed a higher standard of living, with higher wages and lower taxes than in Britain, the economics of that Empire again highlighted the illogical nature of the colonial relationship. All the colonies accepted, as a practical necessity, control of imperial trade by Parliament and the very fact of colonial status implied dependence, and yet the Empire was also built upon the guaranteed existence of representative institutions which implied equality of powers. What often seemed ungrateful, even hostile, actions on the part of colonial legislatures, especially in matters of defence or trade, created resentment in ministerial circles and provoked reminders that such assemblies were dependent on royal authority. Whig ministers approved wholeheartedly of representative institutions, insisting on their introduction into Nova Scotia in 1758[11] but ignoring or forgetting what representative institutions implied about the relationship of colonies with Parliament. Nonetheless there is no reason why illogical relationships should necessarily fail. Neither Nova Scotia nor Jamaica rebelled in 1776.

Although the colonies were therefore dependencies, by 1754 they had already escaped many of the leading strings supposedly held by the hand of Westminster and the pull of authority had dwindled. To some extent the answer to why British authorities allowed this situation to develop lay in the nature of colonial society.

With a population in 1754 of some one and a half million whites, the colonies had developed into a sophisticated, wealthy community with its own customs, developing commerce and burgeoning industries, despite the restrictions imposed by London, and a restless westward expansion was to set the tone of American society for another century. Fishing, shipbuilding, tobacco, distilling and iron-founding were among the main industries. The populations of the eastern seaboard cities of Boston (20 000), New York (18 000), Philadelphia (30 000) and their satellite towns were beginning to grow more rapidly. Unlike Nova Scotia and Newfoundland, whose tiny populations feared the proximity of French neighbours, or Jamaica, where slaves formed 94 per cent of the population, the thirteen colonies could afford to have a certain sense of independence which manifested itself not least in the cavalier attitude taken by merchants and distillers to the prohibitive duty of sixpence per gallon on imported foreign molasses and sugar imposed by Walpole's 1733 Molasses Act. Smuggling, bribery and customs collusion were necessary to New England's distillers and the merchants had the money and ships to secure what they wanted.

Equally central to the origins of independence was the extent to which colonial assemblies had developed away from control by Crown authority. This was in part a consequence of the structure and philosophy of American society, and of 'salutary neglect' by a dominant Treasury, but independence also owed quite a lot to the domination of British politics by that alliance of great families and their dependents, the Old Corps of Whigs, and the development largely but not exclusively at their hands of the concept of parliamentary sovereignty.

Whig Politics and 'salutary neglect'

The idea that ultimate authority lay with the King in Parliament, the balancing forces of monarchy, aristocracy and the 'democratic' element of the Commons, would not have been understood by the politicians and country gentlemen of the reigns of William and Mary and its implications were not perhaps fully understood at the accession of George III. It is doubtful if the elder Pitt ever accepted such an idea completely. In the years after 'The Glorious Revolution' King and Parliament, particularly the Commons, were seen as opposing forces, the executive ever seeking to extend its authority, the lower house in response seeking to challenge rather than co-operate. Such antagonism, because it was seen as potentially dangerous, was never total and, slowly, circumstances and individuals wrought a change in the relationship. Sir Robert Harley, Speaker and later Lord Treasurer, sought co-operation through management, hoping to offset the destructive forces of party; the Junto hoped that party itself and its manipulation of patronage would be the means of co-operation, because the Crown was a necessary ally in the creation of a Court and Treasury bridge between legislature and executive. The latter policy was in the end to prove successful, not because of any special virtues of the Whig party but because George I's accession brought to the throne a monarch who decided, partly for fear of Jacobitism, partly to secure the interests of Hanover, that the Whigs and not the Tories should be his ministers, a view even more vigorously held by his successor. Tory divisions and Jacobitism, practical, sentimental or an admixture, added to the motives which led to single-party Whig administration, with fleeting exceptions until 1760. Such security of tenure enabled Whigs to take full advantage of the patronage resources of the Crown. Its use was hardly novel nor was the increase in the size of the Court and Treasury party particularly great, from c. 120 in 1714 to c. 180 in 1742,[12] but single-party government made patronage much more valuable to the minister and more sought after by the recipient. The Old Corps of Whigs, consisting of placemen, dependents of ministerial allies, seekers after place and benefits for themselves or friends and relations, plus, no doubt, admirers of Walpole or his successors Henry Pelham and Newcastle, dominated administration in the 40 years before George III's accession. Ability, royal favour, patronage, loyalty and the support of a major part of the political and social élite secured this position.

It was hardly likely that the dominant political group would believe other than that the existing order of things was the best. Whig principles underwent a considerable metamorphosis in the years after 1688. J. P. Kenyon has shown how Whigs quietly abandoned contract theories of the origins of government and adapted Tory ideas of non-resistance to the new establishment of limited monarchy which functioned after 1688.[13] The Whigs, quite against the evidence, assumed all credit for 1688, and if 1688 and 1714 secured that happy Protestant, limited monarchy which was the guarantee of an Englishman's liberties, small wonder that Whigs came to argue that resistance to it could not easily be justified, especially if its main enemy was the Tory emphasis on royal authority, whether or not associated with the restoration of the exiled and Catholic Stuarts. 'From King James II's banishment, deposition, or whatever people please to call it I date the birth of real liberty in this kingdom', wrote Lord Hervey in 1734 while Lord Northington was to 'seek for the liberty and constitution of this kingdom no further back than the Revolution'.[14]

The harmony of relations between King, Lords and Commons was seen to lie in the balance of forces it represented. 'The Crown is dependent upon the Commons by the power of granting money; the Commons are dependent on the Crown by the power of dissolution.'[15] Walpole's disingenuous description of this particular element of the balance demonstrates how the Whigs developed the idea that the balance of the three elements preserved liberty, reflected the nation's true interests and therefore should be sovereign. With this went a justification of the influence of the Crown. 'The King must have his real power, as well as the other parts of the legislature and . . . he can have no real power . . . but by these dependencies which his power of disposing of all places . . . creates' (London Journal 1734).[16] Government was still the King's and he must have means to exert his power, but the Commons would check any tendency to tyranny while the Lords would help protect the Crown's powers by checking the Commons' 'democratic' tendencies. By 1760 parliamentary sovereignty was almost universally accepted by the élite as right in itself, as the guardian of English liberties and as of long standing.

This triumph of conservative Whiggism in the hand of the Old Corps was accompanied by a decline, certainly in Parliament, of that older tradition of Whiggism, which saw 1688 as an unfinished revolution, feared power in whoever's hands it lay, and detested influence over the Commons exercised with the assistance of a body of placemen. After the deaths of John Trenchard and Thomas Gordon this 'Commonwealth Whiggism', derived from the Civil War and Exclusion Crisis, made only fitful appearances, considerably tempered, in country opposition to the prevailing Court Whiggism, and even then often merely a rhetorical weapon rather than a genuine programme. It was to be in America that this tradition was to remain alive and where warfare between Governor and legislature remained central to political life, giving American Whiggism a different flavour, and the conflict with Parliament more than a whiff of the seventeenth century.

12

The Whigs who dominated politics in the reigns of the first two Georges adapted Whiggism to power, borrowed much Tory doctrine and developed the idea of parliamentary sovereignty. Locke's Whiggism was rejected for the more utilitarian version of Hume, and from Locke came only the idea that government was created to preserve the natural right of property. 'Our men of property', said Chancellor Hardwicke in 1754, 'are our only free men according to the meaning of the word among the old Grecians and Romans.'[17] Such an emphasis was natural to men who presided over an increasingly oligarchic political system. According to John Cannon one in six adult English males was entitled to vote in 1754[18] but this has to be seen in the context of the Septennial Act, the progressive decline in the number of contested elections, the property qualification for MPs and the social connections between the two Houses outlined by John Cannon in *Aristocratic Century*.[19] Walpole, Pelham and Newcastle presided over a parliamentary system managed by a narrow landowning, even narrowly aristocratic, élite with members of the Lords controlling the election of 170 MPs by 1754. Defenders of the system pointed out that all men were virtually represented in that the social or economic interest of which they were a part was represented in Parliament, as the colonists indeed were. Even so, the contrast with American representative practice is startling.

Such conservative and social and political élitism was not the result solely of Whig or Old Corps domination of politics. The Tory party, Jacobite or not, was committed to the pursuit of political power and there is no evidence that their interests were any less exclusive. Moreover J. C. D. Clark's lively work has underlined convincingly the conservative nature of English society, with the majority committed to a view of social and political obligations far closer to the patriarchal world of the early Stuarts than to the liberal one of the last Hanoverians.[20]

Throughout the eighteenth century the idea that a constitution existed for the preservation of liberties and for facilitating the effectiveness of authority was commonplace. To the Whigs the Crown, whose authority was essential to social order, was potentially dangerous unless limited by a Whig House of Commons and a strong ministry. To Tories the King's power, the fountainhead of all secular authority under God, used extensively by an over-powerful minister possessing the tools of money and place, could equally destroy the constitution. Either way the executive was seen as essential but latently tyrannical, and in opposition Whigs and Tories adopted country attitudes which perpetuated the idea that the real constitution should be a balance of power, though like all those who talk of a balance of power, what each meant was a favourable imbalance. The balance was to be preserved from the interference of King or Crown and the confusion between the two was not unravelled in this period. 'King in Parliament' seems to have acquired the old prerogatives of the monarch. But it also needed to be protected from the influence of 'democratic' pressure, hence the refusal to allow publication of debates and, perhaps, the steady erosion of electoral independence. Such a defence of the independence of the House of Commons and of the idea of the balance of the constitution increased the prevalence of the idea of parliamentary sovereignty while at the same time inhibiting a full understanding of the authority which underlay the concept. [The Declaratory Act was an assertion of sovereignty but even more it was an assertion of the traditional authority of a patriarchal society whose attitudes to parliamentary and royal authority were still confused and contradictory.] Thus parliamentary sovereignty was implicit but not entirely understood. It was seen as both a legitimation of authority and a guarantee of an Englishman's liberties.

That the totality of parliamentary sovereignty was not yet fully understood is demonstrated by contemporary politicians. Newcastle, in notes for a speech in 1766, could write: 'Colonies not the object of taxation; I am much against taxation. Wales never taxed, till they were represented ... Ireland conquered – Act of Parliament to bind Ireland. Yet no Act can bind in point of Taxes, or Subsidy'[21] and Hardwicke was not prepared to risk a constitutional crisis over assembly objections to Townshend's idea of an Act of Parliament forcing them to furnish salaries for Governors: 'As they are Legislative Bodies I see no help for it.'[22] The Whigs were suspicious of taxation without representation, respected representative institutions, and had earlier in the century rejected plans for a Stamp Duty as constitutionally improper.[23] The origins of 'salutary neglect' and the later Rockinghamite policies of conciliation lay not simply in pusillanimity but also in Whig tradition. That generation of politicians encompassing Walpole, Pelham and Newcastle was not ready for a parliamentary reform of the colonial system. To do so might not only interfere with the royal prerogative but might also, paradoxically, increase the strength of the Crown's position in the colonies at the expense of assemblies and Parliament. This underlies yet again the confusion of thought which underlay the constitutional relationships within the Empire and helps to explain why English and Americans would find it so difficult to cope with clarification and reform. And it should also put us on our guard against assuming that English politicians in general began the conflict with America's legislatures committed to an authoritarian view of Parliament's rights.

Work on British and American political thought and practice in the eighteenth century has emphasised the distinctiveness of the colonial experience. It is clear that the United States' political tradition has been less patrician than that in Britain, emphasising inalienable rights of individuals, asserting popular rather than legislative sovereignty and cultivating a disrespect for political authority. But while many of these traits are visible before 1776 their *triumph* could be as much the result as the cause of the quarrel with Britain and we must be careful not to fall into the trap of ascribing inevitability to the breach.

As we have seen in Britain the views of republican, or commonwealth, Whigs had faded into insignificance by 1730 and patriot Whigs were frequently compromised by the lure of office. Court Whiggism, as detailed by H. T. Dickinson and Reed Browning, rejected the idea of social contract as the basis of social and political order, emphasising the importance of law, Hardwicke's 'standard and guardian of liberty', excusing the imperfections of the political system on the grounds that this reflected the 'excellencies and imperfections' in man himself and warning of the dangers of democracy and too much liberty. The right of resistance was considerably curtailed by this emphasis on order, though never extinguished, and the Whigs, especially those involved in the distribution of offices, saw benefit in defending the prerogative of the Crown.

Country and patriot opposition thrived on fear of corruption and the influence of moneyed men and the Court, and a country platform was developed by men such as Bolingbroke. But though it survived throughout the reigns of George I and George II, it never broke through the bounds of Whig–Tory conflict and such patriots who achieved office did so on Court terms, like Pitt in 1746 and 1757. Such patriot oppositions were largely fruitless and much of their supposed popularity in the country is now doubted too. Court Whigs were anathema to Tories but the emphasis on duty, obedience, order and royal prerogative cannot have failed to touch chords in Tory hearts. The tone of English society, outside a few untypical communities beloved of Marxist historians, was hierarchical, obedient, conservative and traditional, and there was no demonstrable desire on the part of the English people for change. The denizens of Cannock Chase, Kingswood and other troublesome areas of social protest showed no interest in political reform, though they did demonstrate a degree of Jacobitism at times. Redress of grievances was almost always sought initially by legal means and few local complaints achieved a national dimension. To those familiar with religious dissent and radicalism in the seventeenth and late eighteenth centuries the failure of these particular dogs to bark in the reigns of the first two Georges is puzzling. Tories, however much they might have disliked Whigs, were not likely to take up the cause of religious, political or social dissent. A country platform based on opposition to a standing army, placemen, stock jobbers and the influence of Hanover or support for shorter parliaments could make little headway in a century which still saw government as the King's and understood no acceptable way of opposing his chosen ministers. Support for James III might threaten stability in certain circumstances but did not imply a desire for radical constitutional changes; while the Poor Law, religious toleration, the slow pace of economic change, legislation protective of working men, and a responsive landed class kept social strains within bounds.

Of course society was not static nor entirely satisfied with the political system it laboured under, for, after all, the demands for change found in George III's reign did not spring from nowhere, but British society on the eve of the American troubles was not dissatisfied with its lot and maintained a robust patriotism.

Studies of American thought and practice have emphasised its democratic nature, in stark contrast to the British system. Bernard Bailyn, John Brewer and J. R. Pole have detailed the way that American political thought found sustenance in the very seventeenth-century political theorists rejected by the prevailing mood in Britain. Milton, Sidney, Harrington and Locke were the favoured authors, while the writings of late 'republican' Whigs such as Molesworth, Trenchard and Gordon were admired. These authors laid emphasis on separation of government powers, on the right of resistance to tyrannical authority, on the 'fundamental laws and rules of the constitution which ought never to be infringed' (John Adams), and where the British emphasised the need to balance power and liberty Americans tended to stress their usual incompatibility. The constitution existed to preserve liberty or the 'natural rights' of Englishmen, rights which colonists even before 1763 saw threatened in Britain by executive power, luxury and corruption.[24]

As British thought and practice moved towards the concept of parliamentary sovereignty colonial ideas were far closer to an idea of the sovereignty of the people, and thus

J. J. Zubly, delegate from Georgia to the Continental Congress and later a Loyalist, could write that Parliament 'can no more make laws which are against the constitution and the inalienable privileges of British subjects than it can alter the constitution itself', sentiments echoed in 1761 by Otis during the writs of assistance controversy over the rights of individuals and the powers of customs officers, which is discussed below. Although the reluctance of Whig politicians in the reign of George II to tax the colonists suggests that the sense of inalienable rights clearly existed in Britain too, most establishment Whigs were moving towards the idea that rights and liberties were best preserved by the sovereignty of 'King in Parliament'; and while few leading colonists subscribed in an absolute sense to the sovereignty of the people, when pushed into definitions of principle most colonists would take the view that liberty depended on a watchful sovereign people and that power corrupts all those who wield it.

The popular element in the political practice of the colonies was much greater than in England and legislatures more genuinely representative of the will of constituents. New England representatives were selected in town meetings and they were held to be delegates of their constituents and directly accountable. Such meetings could be manipulated by radicals like Sam Adams and Otis but the popular will was always strong. In Britain the MP was not a direct representative of his constituents but, at least in theory, an independent delegate of the whole nation, voting according to conscience and national interest. Outside New England practice was often a great deal less populist but franchises were wide and representatives closely bound by local interest. Such ideas were reinforced by the dissenter origins of many northern colonies, by frontier experience and by a prosperity which avoided extremes of wealth and poverty.

However, just as we should be careful not to assume that all politicians at Westminster understood the logical implications of parliamentary sovereignty or would have chosen to follow them even if they had, so we should also be wary of assuming that there existed in the colonies a belief in popular sovereignty, clearly articulated, fully comprehended and just waiting to be activated by the exercise of its Westminster antithesis.

It is conceivable that the preference for commonwealth Whiggism as a theoretical basis for colonial opposition was the result as much as the cause of the conflict with Parliament, a language and philosophy with which to cloak the immediate and practical needs of opposition to a real threat. The Enlightenment did not cause the French Revolution but its many protagonists provided intellectual justification and language for different stages of the revolution's progress. In America in the eighteenth century constant quarrels between Governors and assemblies kept the conflict between executive and legislature at the forefront of colonial politics. Assertion of power through legislatures over questions of proprietorial rights, salaries, appropriations or the desire of the Virginia House of Burgesses to secure regular meetings and alter the franchise, to say nothing of assembly irritation at the exercise of authority by the Crown's servants in Westminster, was bound to be expressed in the same language as that used by the House of Commons opposition in the reign of William III and occasionally by patriot oppositions in the reigns of the first two Georges. It was inevitable, and it kept Old Whiggism alive in the colonies in a way no longer necessary in Britain, where relations between executive and legislature were reaching a fruitful symbiosis.

The legislatures in the colonies could and did seek popular support but it must be clear that this did not imply a desire to share power. Although colonial society and politics were more 'democratic', the colonies were still run by a self-perpetuating oligarchy, dominating assembly and gubernatorial politics, and the use of essentially democratic ideas to defend oligarchic pretensions without cynicism or self-deception and with a clear awareness of the risk should not surprise us. The legislatures of the colonies were dominated by narrow oligarchies determined to preserve their power and status.

In Massachusetts the voting qualification for electing a representative was the equivalent in modern money of two pounds and 57 pence; in Pennsylvania it was 50 acres of county land or a town freehold worth £50; in Virginia 25 acres with a house or 100 without was the franchise. In all three colonies the eastern seaboard possessed a disproportionate amount of political power and in Virginia, the Carolinas and Pennsylvania full political rights or civil benefits were denied the frontiersmen by the dominant élite. 'No taxation without representation' was a slogan of domestic colonial politics too, and George III's reign marked a growth in radical opposition which placed colonial oligarchies between the Scylla of parliamentary assaults on their control of independent assemblies and the Charybdis of radical assaults on their social and political authority. The élite in Massachusetts was mercantile, centred on Boston and its satellite towns; in Pennsylvania it was an oligarchy of merchants and gentry; in Virginia the gentry, organised in a federation of county oligarchies, dominated politics, wielding influence over a deferential electorate. In all three, religious disabilities operated. In most cases, despite their mutual antipathy, it was to be as allies of the oligarchy that 'patriot' and radical parties led by such as Patrick Henry, James Otis and Samuel Adams were to wage war on Westminster and only at the end of the struggle did such politicians briefly threaten to become the dominant element in colonial politics.

Britain and her colonies both were dominated by oligarchies; in Britain that oligarchy was conservative, Court-centred, aristocratic and very wary of any popular participation in politics. In the colonies, however, the élites lacked titles and the Governor was in no position to create or maintain a large Court party. The élites largely adhered to a common set of codes and principles, libertarian and democratic. A wider but still manipulated electorate could be useful in the conflicts of the legislatures with the Governor, and there had been no reduction in the size of the electorate as in Britain. Should the British oligarchy seek to assert its will in the colonies it would fire the resistance of another oligarchy, recently victorious. Equally, should the colonial oligarchy appear to challenge the recently triumphant British oligarchy it would meet with similar resistance. Tensions within the imperial system which could exacerbate such a situation were plentiful but it would have been thought absurd by most people on both sides of the Atlantic in 1754 that Britain or her colonies could benefit from a breach. Conflicts between colonies over trade or frontiers were more serious and more common than conflict between colonies and the mother country. The idea of America hardly yet existed.

It would seem that the relationship between the old country and the colonies was rather a muddle, but if that relationship was open, untidy and pragmatic it reflected the way Britain was governed in the eighteenth century. The aim of government was tranquillity at home and in the colonies. In the eighteenth century Britain was governed in the same way that class or school is controlled, by a judicious combination of authority and concession or compromise. Force could be used but tempered with lenity; force in the form of the military was always a last resort. Government did not possess the means or the desire to impose central control or the sovereign will of Parliament where it would offend important interests or conflict with ancient liberties. The colonies were similarly treated. There was always the potential for conflict. Practices and philosophies of government were diverging; the colonies were developing a will of their own. In the creation of the idea of parliamentary sovereignty which had largely, if temporarily, calmed constitutional conflicts between executive and legislature in Britain, the colonies had played no part and they were unlikely to accept that Parliament could wield the prerogatives of the Crown anew when they had their own assemblies which had tamed the King's representative. On the other hand, the British were unlikely to accept a challenge to that sovereignty, especially if it also involved economic and diplomatic catastrophe. So, clearly there were potential dangers. But eighteenth-century politicians sought tranquillity and pragmatism, not conflict and ideology. The ruling élite on both sides of the Atlantic had too much to lose by conflict. Nevertheless, conflict there was, and its origins lie in the events following the death of Henry Pelham and the outbreak of the Seven or – in the colonies – Nine Years' War (1754/6–63).

Parties in Flux 1754–63

The obvious difference between the politics of George III's reign and those of his grandfather George II lies in the contrast between the fractious politics and ministerial instability of the former and the domination of political life of the latter by the Old Corps of Whigs in office and an opposition largely formed by the Tory party. This profound change developed between the death of Henry Pelham in 1754 and the resignation of Bute in 1763.

Pelham's death heralded a period of sixteen years during which no minister acceptable to the King and the Commons and dominant in the Treasury could be found to maintain that parliamentary stability created by Sir Robert Walpole. The Duke of Newcastle, Pelham's brother, secured the Treasury but his attempt to govern the Commons through a nonentity, Sir Thomas Robinson, failed in the face of joint opposition by rivals Pitt and Henry Fox. Although Newcastle secured Fox's assistance and dismissed Pitt, he was faced with problems which he could not so easily solve. By 1756 the Prince of Wales was of age and Leicester House, his political base, had re-entered the political fray in opposition to the King's ministers and been led by Bute into alliance with Pitt. Newcastle proved unable to reunite the royal family. Moreover Fox's patron, the Duke of Cumberland, evoked hysterical fear at Leicester House. The outbreak of war complicated the Duke's situation further.

Conflict with France began in earnest in America in 1754 and brought only defeats, like those of Washington (1754) and Braddock (1755). This weakened Newcastle's political position in an obvious way but it also brought Cumberland, as army commander, into the cabinet, increasing the hostility of Leicester House and providing ammunition for Pitt. Newcastle's attempts to prevent war in the colonies escalating into a war in Europe for which he had as yet not secured his preferred Austrian alliance were actively countered by Cumberland and Fox.

When his coup – the Convention of Westminster with Frederick the Great – provoked the very war it was meant to neutralise and Admiral Byng failed to save Minorca from the French, Newcastle, panicked by public reaction, resigned.

Nothing proves the continued unity and power of the Old Corps more than the inability of the Pitt–Devonshire ministry to survive without the acquiescence of Newcastle and his supporters. Detested in the Closet, unable to raise money in the City where the Duke's allies held sway, supported by only a portion of Tory MPs and City radicals, urged by Bute to make peace with Newcastle and limited by Devonshire's desire to resign, the Pitt–Devonshire ministry could not use the Minorca enquiry to pillory the old ministers, many of whom were still in the administration. Its dismissal was little minded, despite the myth of the 'rain of gold boxes'[25]; eventually what all saw as inevitable, an alliance of Pitt and Newcastle, which also united the dynasty, was completed in July 1757.

This ministry which so successfully fought the Seven Years' War also seemed to solve the ministerial instability which had followed Pelham's death. It did no such thing. The brief period between Pelham's death and the emergence of the alliance between Pitt and Newcastle underlined the need for the chief Treasury minister and leader of the Old Corps to be in the House of Commons. Luckily for the Duke, Pitt did not challenge Newcastle's control of the Treasury or the Old Corps, but the alliance only disguised the fact that the Duke could not effectively control the Commons, at least in wartime, without an ally and that he had no ally within the Old Corps fit to do the job. There was no heir to the leadership of the Old Corps. Pitt, uninterested in party, patronage or Treasury was not the man. Nor was Fox, detested by the future King. Moreover, relations between Newcastle and Pitt were increasingly tense, for Pitt never seriously considered the difficulties Newcastle faced raising supply and despised the means by which the Duke maintained support in Parliament.

In 1760 when George II died Newcastle was already 67 years old; the new King was 22. With no political heirs and hated by the new King, Newcastle's political future was likely to be short and bleak. Many of the Old Corps would, of course, remain loyal to Newcastle; others would transfer their hopes to Pitt, temporarily if they were wise; yet more would take a hard look at loyalty and future prospects. The hatred felt by Bute and the King towards Pitt and Newcastle were equally vital considerations. The accession of any new King created political change in the eighteenth century but the circumstances of 1760 made it more resemble 1714 than 1727.

The accession of George III at a time when there was no obvious future leader of the Old Corps threatened that body with dissolution into faction. The circumstances of first Pitt's and then Newcastle's resignations hastened the process. The extraordinary ruthless 'Massacre of the Pelhamite Innocents', the mass dismissal of loyal Newcastle supporters in 1762 by Fox, at the behest of Bute, largely completed the process.

What helped to make political fragmentation even more complete, however, was the disappearance of the Tory party. Whether one believes, with Linda Colley,[26] that the party's disintegration postdates George III's accession or prefers the views of Eveline Cruickshanks and J. C. D. Clark[27] that the party's disappearance is associated with the death of Jacobitism and occurred between 1754 and 1757, no one doubts that the Tory party, as an organised unit within the House of Commons, had disappeared by 1762, most of its members continuing as independent country gentlemen, some, more ambitious, drifting into Whig factions, as did William Dowdeswell into the Rockinghams.

Despite this state of flux a new order and stability might

have been created if Bute, having defeated the Old Corps and passed the Peace Treaty of 1763, secure in the wholehearted support of the Closet, had not quit the field of battle and left the King in the lurch. A period of coalitions and instability now became much more likely.

This new situation was likely to affect American policy in several ways. This is not, however, because ministerial instability created deeply differing views among political factions on America for, as we have already seen, British politicians were largely united in their belief in parliamentary sovereignty and their preference for pragmatism. The trend towards faction created a need for coalition; ministers did not change *en bloc*, continuity was considerable and pragmatism prevented too many switches of policy. Only in 1765 with the Rockinghams' desire to discredit Grenville did faction directly influence policy, and even there only marginally. It is true that America was an issue which created 'badges of difference' between politicians but Grafton, a friend of America and a member of the ministry which had repealed the Stamp Act, allied himself with Bedford who had been Grenville's ally in passing it and never ceased to support that policy. Perhaps faction did inhibit coherent American policies, but it is worth recalling that North's united, popular and powerful ministry was the one which actually provoked the Declaration of Independence.

The end of the stability of George III's reign did, however, influence American policy. Ministers were bound to have to pay greater attention to the independents whose views were generally very conservative and thoroughgoing where America was concerned. The collapse of the Old Corps, accompanied as it was by the death or retirement of the politicians of the generation of Newcastle and Hardwicke, made it unlikely that the policy of 'salutary neglect' would continue, in the context of the Seven Years' War and a younger, less amenable, generation of politicians whose political apprenticeship was not influenced by the politics of Queen Anne's reign. George III's less 'germanick' outlook and his constitutional correctness provided an additional support to the defence of the rights of Parliament against those who challenged it, while his undeserved reputation for 'tyranny' would provide ammunition for those who sought to oppose the policy of taxing the colonies.

The Nine Years' War 1754–63

British politicians found themselves in a new situation in their relationships with the colonies as well as at Westminster. The Nine Years' War led to a series of conflicts with the British government and its agents in which constitutional strains inherent in the system became starkly visible.

In 1754 the Albany Conference met, initiated by the British government to try to secure more effective inter-colonial resistance to French encroachments and a common Indian policy. Some delegates, especially Benjamin Franklin, sought to widen the discussions to include a form of inter-colonial union, an idea favoured initially by Newcastle. Unfortunately for Franklin a change of mind on the govern-ment's part and resistance on the part of several colonial legislatures to any diminution of their authority ruined his plans. Massachusetts saw it as a parliamentary scheme 'of gaining power over the colonies' and Rhode Island feared 'a power above law, over the several legislatures'.

The scene was set for a series of quarrels in which the rights of colonial legislatures would be asserted against the perceived requirements of British War policy. Pennsylvania opposed the appointment of William Johnson as Superinten-dent of North Indian Affairs in 1755 and objected to his peace with the Delaware nations in 1756. General Amherst also fell foul of Pennsylvania's assembly over Indian affairs in 1758. The Pontiac rising of 1763 confirmed the colonists' belief that British interference in an area of policy properly belonging to the assemblies was wrong. Even more they came to see the increased military presence on the frontiers after the war as provocative and sinister.

The attempts by the army to impress and recruit during

the war led not only to mob resistance in cities such as Boston, but also to protests by assemblies against 'an unconstitutional and arbitrary invasion of our rights and properties' (Pennsylvania).[28] Americans fiercely resisted quartering of redcoats on their property. When ordered by the Governor to quarter British soldiers Pennsylvania's opposition was led by Franklin and the assembly refusing to abide by the provisions of the Mutiny Acts. Similar opposition was found in Massachusetts and New York. The Earl of London, Commander-in-Chief (1756–7), reported that it was 'from the leading people who raise the dispute in order to have merit with the others by defending their liberties, as they call them'. The generals' belief that they and not the colonial assemblies should determine the provincial contribution to the war led to bitter conflicts between generals and Governors on one side and assemblies on the other.

The war also created friction by the necessary restrictions imposed on colonial trade. Soon, methods used by the Royal Navy and the Commander-in-Chief to stamp out smuggling were said to deny the rights of Englishmen. In general, assemblies did not agree to an embargo on trade with French or neutral ports but the issue of writs of assistance which brought James Otis to prominence in Massachusetts' radical circles helped unleash a new resistance. Otis, in 1761, challenged the validity of such documents acquired by customs officers from the courts to enable them to search for contraband. Backed by merchants, Otis argued before the Superior Court sitting in the Boston Town House that an Act of Parliament 'against the constitution is void'. According to the alarmed John Adams he asserted the doctrine that 'everyman . . . was an independent sovereign, subject to no law, but the law written on his heart'. This was rhetorical nonsense but Otis's chief argument raised the question of Parliament's sovereignty in a way popular with most colonial élites. The Pennsylvanian assembly asserted that '. . . a People cannot be said to be free . . . when their rulers shall by their sole authority, even during the Sitting of their Assemblys stop the circulation of Commerce'.[29]

The war also affected British attitudes to the colonists. To British observers their contribution to self-defence had been grudging, and colonial legislatures insular and troublesome. This was hardly fair to Massachusetts which had been generous with money and men, but Massachusetts was exceptional. Lack of co-operation between colonies or with the British regulars seemed from the British point of view almost treasonable. 'No one in this country can be relied upon', wrote Colonel Bosquet of the Pennsylvanians, while Wolfe referred to American regulars as 'the most contemptible cowardly dogs you can conceive',[30] a view of the American fighting man which was to encourage thoughts of easy British victory in 1775. The inadequacies of the American regulars and the difficulties experienced in raising regular colonial forces obliged the army command to rely more heavily on regulars sent from Britain, which increased Parliamentary responsibility and the burden the war placed on the British tax-payer. Charles Jenkinson pointed out that the increased tax burden on the British people by 1762 was £1 400 000 annually.[31]

Whether or not American smuggling did prolong the war is open to question, but the niceties of such an argument would have been lost on the English country gentleman who simply saw colonists trading with the enemy. The colonists' wish to keep Indian relations in the hands of the legislatures could be, not unfairly, ascribed to the greed of speculators and competing commercial interests.

The wars left the British and the colonists on bad terms. Whatever the truth of the accusations which each side might level at the other, the colonists felt that British authorities had attempted to ride roughshod over their liberties and failed to treat their assemblies with proper respect. Oligarchies and popular elements could make common cause against the effects of British war policies. To the British the colonists could appear selfish, insular, cowardly and high-handed in their constitutional pretensions. Above all the war was seen as having been fought on behalf of the colonists at great expense, an oversimplification challenged by Franklin later but nevertheless genuinely believed. The increase of parliamentary and financial responsibility for the colonies – the National Debt doubled to £140 000 000 during the War – seemed to require a more effective control of the Empire by Parliament. The need was there and the opportunity was afforded by French defeat, a defeat which also released the colonists from one of the factors which had always dictated prudence in their relations with Westminster.

2

1760–70: PRINCIPLE AND PRAGMATISM

According to young Thomas Jefferson writing in his pamphlet *A Summary View of the Rights of America* in 1774 the colonies were the victim of 'a series of oppressions, begun at a distinguished period, and pursued unalterably through every change of ministers, [which] too plainly prove a deliberate systematical plan of reducing us to slavery'. One of the purposes of the next chapter is to enquire whether there is any truth at all in this polemic and to study the motives and principles of the main British politicians.

The main events of the years 1760 to 1770 are well enough known but it will be useful to remind ourselves of the chronology. George III's reign began in the midst of war with France and the inexperienced monarch made no attempt to change his ministers at first. But Newcastle's unhappiness at his loss of favour in the Closet with the favour shown to Bute, and his unhappy relations with Pitt, created one source of ministerial disintegration, and Pitt's refusal to be Bute's friend and ally another. Pitt's resignation over cabinet refusal to make a pre-emptive strike against Spain and Newcastle's over the withdrawal of credit for Frederick the Great led Bute to the office of First Lord of the Treasury in May 1762, a position which he did not wish to take, preferring always to have influence without responsibility, and from which he resigned in 1763.

Bute's brief period as First Lord saw the passing of the Treaty of Paris, 1763, which ended the war with France, and the new First Lord had already turned his mind to the colonial question before obliging the King first to turn to Fox and then George Grenville, equally obnoxious in the King's eyes, as his successor.

Bute's administration had already decided to station part of the army permanently in America at the end of the war and to have it paid for by the colonists. This was partly a response to the terrifying rise of the National Debt and partly to the renewed threat on the frontier from the Indians, signalled by Pontiac's rebellion in 1763. Similarly the decision to keep a naval squadron in America, at Halifax, for the first time had the double purpose of improving colonial defence and making the suppression of smuggling more effective. Grenville had been party to these decisions and for reasons of his own he was likely to advance their general direction.

The character and disposition of 'Mr Greenvile' materially influenced the policy and history of this ministry. Grenville's career had been overshadowed by his elder brother, Earl Temple, and brother-in-law, Pitt. His ambition had been fed by disappointment at missing promotions in 1746, 1749, 1754 and particularly 1757. He refused the Exchequer under Bute in 1761 and when he became First Lord he was determined to establish his authority against Bute, whose creature he was perceived to be, against his relations and if need be against the King. The King detested Grenville and still sought the advice of Bute behind Grenville's back. The history of the administration is one of crises in relations with the King. But if Grenville was weak in the Closet, he was soon powerful in Parliament. The King found it impossible to get rid of Grenville in June or August 1763, for he could as yet find no alternative and the ministry was strengthened by the acquisition of Bedford's group, but above all Grenville with 'the mind of a counting house clerk' (Horace Walpole) endeared himself to the country gentlemen by the vigour

31

with which he attacked the most alarming problem of the day, the size of the National Debt; and here America was to play a large part in establishing his reputation for sound financial administration and defending the interests of Parliament.

Acutely conscious of the size of the debt, anxious to satisfy the country gentlemen, who disliked land tax at four shillings in the pound and were, as we have seen, angry at America's performance in the war, Grenville was also aware of the new Indian threat and therefore he continued Bute's policy. Pontiac's rising in 1763–5, provoked by Amherst, made necessary a temporary measure, the Royal Proclamation Line of 1763. This accepted the general policy of the superintendent of Indian affairs that only by restricting westward expansion could Indian troubles be prevented. The line of the Appalachian watershed was therefore fixed 'for the present' as the limit of British settlement. The measure could be justified; but it upset colonists, who blamed Britain for the massacre of 2000 settlers, and it annoyed important sections of the colonial élite who had ambitious plans for land speculation. Moreover, the line needed policing, and that meant troops and money. It was to the question of money that Grenville now turned.

The subject of how to raise more money from the colonies had been in the air, especially in Board of Trade circles, in Pelham's time; but the Seven Years' War had made it acute. British politicians were influenced by several universally held assumptions; that the National Debt was too high and that further domestic taxes might be ruinous to industry; that a permanent military presence in America was inevitable; that the colonists had smuggled during the war; that they had failed to raise troops of their own or properly support those sent from Britain; and that the American colonists were prosperous and could afford to pay. Already under Bute the administration had looked at the raising of a revenue in America. George III wrote to Lord Bute in March 1763: 'The subject was new to none, having been thought of the whole winter'[1] and he had in theory decided to raise a revenue in America. When the question of renewing the Molasses Act, due to expire in September 1763, arose, the government was interested in the question of whether it could be used to raise a revenue in America. As President of the Board of Trade, Charles Townshend even went so far as to accept the amendment to the Act to reduce the duty to two pence as a first stage. Since 1757 Townshend had urged the need to raise a revenue in America to pay for royal government and soldiers there; but in 1763 he was acting without authority and his triumph was temporary. It is hardly surprising that Grenville, with his counting house mind and his reputation for administrative reform, hard work and economy, should have decided to apply the 'smack of firm government' to America, and there is no doubt that the vigorous prosecution of the policy was very much his though assisted by some able and knowledgeable men.

A few days after becoming First Lord in April 1763 Grenville set to work to tighten up safeguards against illicit trade. The Hovering Act was to be enforced and the customs service in America was reformed. Absentee officers were forced to their posts; the navy was ordered to give full support, and Grenville demanded exact statistics of exports and revenues. By October 1764 he was fully informed of the extent of smuggling. He also sought advice on two possible means of raising revenue. Henry McCulloch of North Carolina and Nathaniel Ware, a former Controller of Customs in Britain, were ordered to enquire, respectively, into a Stamp Bill and a reduction of the Molasses Duty from sixpence per gallon, the idea being not only to make smuggling less profitable but, by removing a prohibitive rate of tax, to make the tax payable; in other words to raise a revenue from, rather than simply to manage, trade.

The result of Ware's work and Grenville's determination was the passage of the Sugar Act (or Plantation Act) which went triumphantly through Parliament in March 1764 with no protest. The Act reduced the duty to threepence, added hides and skins to the list of enumerated articles and imposed duties on certain heavy goods imported into America. But if the opposition in Britain was hardly visible, the political importance of the measure was not lost on the ministry. Thomas Whately, Secretary to the Treasury and formerly Grenville's private secretary, wrote of the duties: 'they are a political regulation. [Enforcement] enforces the observance of those wise laws to which the increase of our trade and naval power are principally owing'.[2] Whately was largely responsible for proposing the Stamp Bill, and as Grenville's lieutenant his views are an important guide to the motive of the administration. It is clear that already ministers feared the tendency of the colonies towards separation and saw that the survival of Britain as a great power relied on the maintenance of colonial dependence. Smuggled trade 'was all stolen from the commerce, and part of it from the manufactures of Great Britain, contrary to the fundamental principle of colonisation, to every maxim of policy, and to the express provision of the law'.[3]

It is also clear that the principle of raising a revenue was crucial to Grenville's ministers, as it had been to Townshend. It was this aspect which raised such a storm in America; for not only was the principle of 'no taxation without representation' being flouted and the rights of colonists and their assemblies overborne, but the Sugar Act was clearly a dry run for a Stamp Act of whose preparation the colonists were fully aware. Moreover, tighter customs regulation and naval high-handedness had already upset merchant interests, affected as they also were by a postwar depression. The assemblies of the colonies prepared their main protests for the Stamp Bill; but in Boston Otis, Jared Ingersoll and other radicals were loud in their protests, while the New York assembly petitioned that 'exemption from ... involuntary taxes must be the grand principle of every free state'.[4]

Such loud protests did not seriously influence Grenville or Whately, though the latter was assiduous in his researches and requests for colonial opinion on his proposals. The Stamp Tax on official papers and transactions would be simple to collect, cheap and unavoidable. It 'is not subject to the frauds to which Custom House duties are liable, nor to the severities of excise ... nor is it necessary to enter any man's doors for the purpose of collecting it'.[5] It is clear from this that Grenville liked the Stamp Duty for its efficiency but also saw it as the least likely tax to raise a storm on libertarian grounds. Nevertheless, it was 'a great measure on account of the important point it establishes, the right of Parliament to levy an internal tax upon the colonies' (Whately).[6]

The Bill was ready by November 1763; but there followed a delay, despite Grenville's assertion that he did believe in 'the right to impose an inland tax' and a hardening of his administration's attitude in the face of American protests; these just had the effect of causing the administration to emphasise increasingly the constitutional aspect of the tax at the expense of the financial. Perhaps Grenville sought to prove that he was prepared to listen to colonial complaints, though he only met colonial agents as a group once, and they failed to convince him either that he was constitutionally in the wrong or that he could rely on the assemblies to supply a revenue of their own goodwill, and it is doubtful whether he would have been deflected from the assertion of right, even if they had.

Grenville's real response to colonial protests was to secure a large majority for his measure in 1765. Whately had done his research well. The duty was to be at a lower rate than the Stamp Duty in England so as not to upset the poorer colonists. There would be protests, Whately was sure; but he and Charles Jenkinson assured the administration that stamp duties always led to protests but that duties would be paid.

Introducing the question of taxing America in February 1765 Grenville went immediately to the central problem of whether Parliament could levy an *internal* tax on the colonies despite 'the general right of mankind not to be taxed but by their representative',[7] which he himself asserted. He agreed that many British people lacked direct representation but were nonetheless taxed; 'the Parliament of Great Britain virtually represents the whole kingdom, not actually the great trading towns'. Virtual representation, the indirect representation of property interests, was to be a key argument in the assertion of Parliament's right to levy an internal tax. 'All colonies', he confidently asserted, 'are subject to the domination of the mother country.' Besides, he argued that the money raised would be spent entirely within America, that the rate was low, that Americans only would be agents and that he had spared no effort to find out 'from North America whether they objected to this particular species of tax . . . and has not heard one gentleman propose any other'. With satisfaction Grenville saw only 49 members vote against the Bill, and that on its first reading only. Thus easily did the Stamp Act, which was to begin the slide towards the loss of the American colonies, pass the House.

The ministry, before its demise, passed one further measure of American policy. The Mutiny Act of May 1765 dealt with the difficulties experienced by the army in America in securing quarters. The measure caused the King distress at the idea of billeting on private houses; and it, far more than the Stamp Act had done, raised the hopes of opposition. Representatives from colonial agents and from 'The Body of Merchants Trading with America' led Grenville to make amendments which satisfied most interests, and the Bill was passed. By July, however, Grenville was out of office.

Grenville fell because the King finally found politicians willing to replace him. Prerogative ousted Grenville and raised Rockingham. The shadow of Bute made Grenville suspicious of the King, avaricious on matters of patronage, and ill at ease in the Closet. His refusal to allow the King to retain Bute as keeper of the King's privy purse (the King's private expenditure), or to allow him to appoint Sir William Breton, a friend, albeit also a Butite, to this household post, exacerbated royal displeasure and did nothing to calm Grenville's fears of being considered merely a stop-gap minister. But it was the Regency Crisis, a sorry tale of mutual non-communication, which provoked the King finally to get rid of his minister.

The King's desire to provide for a Regency while keeping the royal family united – 'to disgust none and to gratify none' (Hardwicke) – provoked fears of Bute's influence among the ministry. The King's failure to express his motives to Grenville and Grenville's inability to express his fears to the King, led to a final collapse of mutual confidence. The King's unsuccessful attempt, through Cumberland, to negotiate a change of ministry with Newcastle's friends in May, an attempt of which the ministry was soon cognisant, led to Grenville and Bedford imposing humiliating terms on the King. Rigby (Bedford's man of business) 'swore a great oath that the King should not have power to appoint one of his own footmen'.[8] It was one of the lowest points of the King's reign: and yet no ministry could long survive on such bad terms with the King, and George III, unlike his grandfather, was not inclined to learn to love what he could not avoid. The problem for George and Cumberland was the unwillingness of many of the friends of Newcastle and Rockingham to come in without Pitt. Luckily for the King, Pitt's – or Temple's – intransigence made the Whigs, gathered at Claremont in July, more willing to risk forming a ministry provided that the King made a few dismissals 'as proof to the world' that Bute had no influence. The King promised that Bute would not interfere and that any Butite opposing the ministry would be dismissed. With that the new men had to be satisfied; 'for they are men who have principles and therefore cannot approve of seeing the Crown dictated to by low men' (George III).[9] Grenville was never again to hold office.

The Rockinghamites were those followers of the Duke of Newcastle who had left administration with, or after, the 'Massacre of the Pelhamite Innocents', particularly the younger aristocrats of the Old Corps, with their friends and relations. Newcastle, increasingly ignored, was no longer its head. It was a coalition of aristocratic families led by Rockingham, Richmond, Portland, Albermarle, the Cavendishes, the Duke of Grafton, General Conway and others of similar birth and persuasion; in almost every sense 'an honourable connection'. The ministry lacked leadership of the first rank in the Commons and initially depended on royal prerogative, the leadership of Cumberland, and the expected acquiescence of 'the King's Friends', a misnamed and far from uniform group of supporters of Bute and good government.

Expectations of its success were significantly absent. Charles Townshend, Paymaster-General since May, described it as 'a lutestring ministry ... fit only for the summer'.[10] The First Lord, Rockingham, 'never rose (to speak) without affording matters of mortification to his friends, and of Triumph to his Enemies'.[11] His inexperience was mirrored by that of Grafton (Secretary of State for the North) and Conway (South) who as Leader of the House was 'so unable, so weak and so indecisive'.[12] Conway could at least count on the competent support in the Commons of Dowdeswell, Chancellor of the Exchequer.

From the beginning this ministry was obsessed by fear of Bute, a desire to undermine Grenville's reputation, and the attitude to it of William Pitt. Dubbed 'Butal-Ducal' by Temple, and described by Bedford as having 'no better foundation than the support of Lord Bute's favouritism',[13] the ministers sought, especially after Cumberland's death in October 1765, to distance themselves from any possible association with Bute, a determination which led directly to bitter relations with the King. The influence of Pitt and Grenville is important for the future history of the Rockinghams and their relations with the King, but equally crucial in its effects on American policy.

Lieutenant-Governor Thomas Hutchinson of Massachusetts, while warning the British government of the anger of the colonists against the Stamp Act, nevertheless wrote that 'there was no other expectation than that the duty would be paid and the Act submitted to', while Benjamin Franklin was so sure of this that he advised a friend to apply for the post of Stamp Duty collector. In fact the response of the colonists was one of bitter protest and controlled violence, particularly after Virginia's adoption of Patrick Henry's Resolves in a half-empty House of Burgesses, largely dominated by up-country members. The four accepted resolutions emphasised that the exclusive right of taxation within Virginia was held by the legislature. Two other rejected resolves, urging resistance and declaring as an enemy anyone who advised acceptance of the tax, were nonetheless taken up in other colonies, especially by Massachusetts on 2 July. But even before that the House of Representatives there had set up a committee of correspondence to consult with other colonial assemblies; and this idea developed, with the agreement of other assemblies, into the Stamp Act Congress which met in October.

A campaign of intimidation with the main aim of stopping the duty being paid, was led by the gentry, merchants and lawyers everywhere, often aided by well-organised mobs of long standing. In Boston the 'Sons of Liberty' emerged from the Caucus Club which had existed for some years, dedicated to the overthrow of the Bernard–Hutchinson oligarchy in Massachusetts politics. Thus radicals seized their opportunity. The burning of the effigy of Andrew Oliver, stamp distributor, on 11 August was the prelude to orchestrated violence and destruction, in which officials of the vice-admiralty courts and customs saw their houses ransacked and Hutchinson's house was wrecked. Similar scenes in other colonies, notably New York, and the reluctance of the authorities, many of whom aided and abetted the troubles, made the Act inoperable, undermined royal government and forced distributors of the stamps to resign. Only in Georgia was it possible to take issue with the popular party.[14] The troubles left behind a dangerous legacy of inter-colonial co-operation and the Sons of Liberty, now to be found in all colonies. Above all the management of the opposition to the Act had given the colonists a taste, albeit limited, of self-government.

The violence of August was seen by many to be counter-productive and it was soon reined in, but 'the weapon with which the Colonies armed themselves to most advantage', wrote Horace Walpole, 'was the refusal of paying the debts they owed to our merchants at home'[15] and in practice an embargo on trade.

The Virginia Resolves were known about in England in July, the troubles in Boston in October, those in New York in

December. The ministry, already busy undoing the reputation of the Grenville ministry by repealing the Cider Excise
and declaring General Warrants illegal, was taken by surprise, and the initial response was mixed. Newcastle foresaw
'very little effect by enforcing the executing of the stamp
duty';[16] Conway ordered 'such a timely Exertion of Force as
occasion may require',[17] but Rockingham on 13 October was
already planning 'to execute [the Act] by fair means not by
military force' and to give the colonies 'some relief' once they
had accepted Parliament's sovereign right to tax.[18] While
Cumberland lived some appeal to force was always possible,
though increasingly it was clear that the government lacked
means, or as good Whigs, inclination. After his death, on 31
October, all such ideas were abandoned.

The administration took time to recover its equilibrium.
On America it sought time and more information and,
briefly, it considered an approach to Pitt to satisfy Grafton
and Conway. But the delay allowed other forces to work on
the development of Rockinghamite policy. Already the
ministry had shown a propensity to react negatively to
Grenville's ministry, and it suited them to repeal or modify
the Stamp Act and to put the blame for the troubles firmly on
Mr Grenville's shoulders. Grenville himself recognised that
'it is intended to attack during the ensuing session of
Parliament almost every Public measure which I promoted
during the two former sessions'.[19] The Rockingham administration was also, however, the heir to the Pelham tradition of
'salutary neglect', summed up in Burke's later argument that
'I am not determining a point of law; I am restoring
tranquillity'.[20]

Delay, however, also permitted agents of the colonies to
make their arguments felt. Franklin in particular was assiduous in his meetings and writings, though he worked for
concessions rather than repeal as more easily to be achieved.
More important, however, were the ministry's links with the
'London North American Merchants Committee' with whose
spokesman Barlow Trecothick Burke was quickly in contact,
possibly at the suggestion of Newcastle. Trecothick had

always opposed the Stamp Act, no doubt influenced by his strong Bostonian and West Indies connections. The merchants were very concerned with the collapse of trade. Bristol, Burke's constituency, petitioned for relief in October, and Trecothick orchestrated from December a petitioning movement which embraced 25 towns and cities by early 1766, and which encouraged the mistaken view that the trade depression of 1765–6 was the direct result of the Stamp Act.

Because the campaign had the blessing of Rockingham and his parliamentary allies, it was likely to have success. This was how any popular pressure group secured what it wanted in the eighteenth century. Certainly it helped Rockingham to prepare for the presentation of a policy of conciliation to Parliament; but it was not until 19 January that the administration finally decided on its two-part American policy: an act declaratory of Parliament's right to legislate in all matters for the colonies, plus repeal. When the ministry met Parliament for the first time on 17 December, little reference was made to America and little enough after Christmas, though a Declaratory Act did become cabinet policy on 27 December. Part of the delay was through fear of what the House would think of concessions to violence; but time was taken up also worrying about Bute's attitude and that of the King's Friends, most of whom were known to oppose any policy involving repeal and most of whom were still in the administration. Time was also taken up seeking Pitt's opinion on America, which he refused to give to anyone but King or Parliament, though his opposition to the Stamp Act was common knowledge, and in attempting once without the King's permission, and once with, to seek Pitt's membership of the administration. His terms were unacceptable, involving as they did the dissolution of the ministry. On the day after the second approach to Pitt the government decided on its policy. That policy came to seem like a response to Pitt's speech of 16 January in which he had insisted on repeal and declared that Parliament had had 'no right to levy an internal tax on America'. This incidentally raised the red herring of a distinction between internal and external taxation, that is taxation through revenue duties which it was presumed occurred already; but its immediate consequence was to determine Bute to oppose repeal. As we have seen, the Rockingham policy had many origins; and the Declaratory Act flatly contradicts Pitt's argument. The most that can be said is that Pitt's speech made the administration more sanguine about its chances.

Proceeding cautiously by resolutions, persuading the House that the economic consequences of the Stamp Act were disastrous and blaming the dangerous level of unemployment, quite falsely, on the troubles with America, the administration argued that the difficulties of enforcement were insurmountable. Lobbying, and providing well-primed witnesses for the enquiry into the disturbances in America and their economic effects, the administration steered discussion away from constitutional issues as much as possible, and distanced itself from Pitt's clearly unacceptable arguments. By juxtaposing a strong declaration that Parliament 'had, hath and of right ought to have full power and authority to make laws and statutes of sufficient form and validity to bind the colonies and people of America in all cases whatsoever' though excluding the original words 'as well in cases of taxation as (in all cases whatsoever)', the administration satisfied the question of right, and by emphasising practical problems and economic disaster convinced enough MPs of the needs of expedience: '... it was the clamour of trade ... that had borne down all opposition'.[21] Pitt's opinions paradoxically helped the administration; 'Mr Pit's (sic) opinion, even Mr Pit's opinion that Great Britain hath no right to tax the Colonies, cannot convince me'[22] was the robust opinion of the MP for Penryn, and Pitt's intervention convinced many MPs that support for the administration was sound sense, especially as the King had declared his support for the policy. Both Bills received the royal assent on 18 March.

The colonial policy of the Rockingham administration did not end with these measures. The Free Port Act established a port in Dominica permitted to trade with foreign colonies, and the American Duties Act repealed Grenville's Sugar Act, allowing molasses into the colonies on payment of a penny duty. The policies were challenged by Pitt, Beckford and the West Indies interest, and Pitt's hostility to the ministry helped Grafton to his resolution to resign on 28 April. Pitt's later change of mind on the penny duty and his retirement to nurse his many ills at Bath enabled the government to proceed to completion and forced Beckford and the West Indies interest to achieve the best deal they could; continued protection for British sugar and concessions on rum. In all the politicking between rival commercial interests few seem to have noted that the new duty on molasses was quite clearly a revenue-raising measure; politicians accepted Franklin's assertion of a distinction between internal and external taxes, made during his cross-examination by the privy council on 28 January, a misleading distinction which was soon to cause renewed mischief.

Rockinghamite colonial policy was largely negative in its concentration on sweeping away Grenville's work. No solution was found to the frontier problem nor to the vexed question of raising a substantial revenue. Whether the Rockinghamites could have achieved anything more positive can only be guessed at, for in July 1766 the ministry was at an end.

The Rockingham administration's demise owed little to America though the Stamp Act featured in the quarrels between King and ministers. It is true that the King would have preferred modification to repeal but his dissatisfaction with his ministers, quite understood by Newcastle whose opinion was that His Majesty was 'weary of an Administration of boys' had many causes which will be discussed below. When Pitt signalled his willingness 'to come if called upon', a new ministry, still perforce based on Rockingham's followers, could be formed. It would remain to be seen if this administration could find a means of solving the chief problem of the colonies; how to raise a revenue and maintain Parliament's rights, as defined by Rockingham's ministry in the Declaratory Act, without arousing more opposition in the colonies than existing resources there could cope with.

The new administration excited hopes almost everywhere. In America it was seen to be captained, and largely officered, by 'Friends of America', though Charles Townshend's presence might have seemed odd, as he was one of the most inveterate opponents of the colonists' constitutional pretensions. To the King, who gave Chatham every possible support, it seemed that he had at last a ministry not founded on factions and capable of withstanding the onslaughts of Grenville. Even to Rockingham the presence in the ministry of many of his friends seemed likely to provide a garrison which might later open the gates to an amicable return of the whole party.

In truth the ministry was from the very beginning prone to disaster. Bute's distress at the scant regard paid by Pitt, or Chatham as he now was, to his followers – 'My heart is half broke' – could largely be discounted. He was soon to go abroad and the King's Friends would remain a reality only in the fevered imagination of the Rockinghamites, but Chatham had made no inroads into the followings of Grenville or Bedford. It is true that he reduced the numbers of Rockinghamites when the Marquis disastrously failed to storm the Closet on the dismissal of one of their number, Lord Edgecumbe, as Treasurer of the Household in November 1766; but the ministry lacked cohesion, while the attempt to extirpate party only made the opposition factions more cohesive. Pitt's determination since 1761 had been to be 'dictator' of any ministry, and no ministry was supposed to function except under those circumstances. Should the dictator fall ill the administration would truly be, as Burke later described it, 'a tesselated pavement.'[23] Conway, who had so often lamented Pitt's absence from Rockingham's administration, now furiously resented the consequences of Edgecumbe's dismissal and the hostility of his erstwhile friends. Grafton lacked the authority to be First Lord, as he was intended to, but this was no recipe for co-operation with a Chancellor of the Exchequer who did not really want the post, which he took largely for a seat in the cabinet and a hoped-for peerage for his wife. His reputation for brilliant irresponsibility seems largely deserved, and his American and East India Company policies were at odds with those of most of his colleagues. Shelburne, Secretary for the South, was universally disliked, though the reasons for this seem now difficult to fathom. It was not, therefore, a ministry designed for co-operative effort. Everything depended on the Earl of Chatham.

Before retiring to Bath for the Christmas period Chatham had accomplished little of importance in policy. He had failed to secure an alliance with Prussia, as anyone with any experience of diplomatic realities could have foretold, and on the issues of India and America his cabinet was divided.

He had, by the end of 1766, largely washed his hands of the American colonists, his conciliatory policy soon changing when New York showed a steadfast refusal to obey the Mutiny Act while Massachusetts indemnified the rioters against the Stamp Act and refused to compensate those in Boston whose property had suffered the attentions of the mob. Convinced that a 'perverse infatuation' had seized the colonists, he seems to have decided that they were not worthy of his attention any more. This left the initiative in American policy at first to Shelburne, who was faced with the issues of frontier and revenue which Rockingham had bequeathed to his successors. Shelburne sought advice from General Gage, commander of the British forces in America, from Lord Barrington, Secretary at War, from Governors and American officials. His solution, arrived at in November, was to allow the colonists to expand westwards and, after initial assistance from the army, to manage the Indian problem themselves, thus allowing the army to concentrate itself on the eastern seaboard. The revenue question was to be solved by 'taking proper care of the quit rents', and in December he required the Governors to inform him how many such rents were being collected and whether they could be more effectively managed. In view of the fact that in 1763 Shelburne had rejected the idea of raising a revenue in this way because of the unpopularity and the practical difficulty involved in collecting them, it is curious that he should have seen this as an answer. But at least no one could deny that such rents were due, in law, to the Crown and that the assemblies could hardly complain. The limitation of the scheme, even if it had ever been possible, was that it was purely for the upkeep of the army and left the problem of the acute weakness of royal administration in the colonies unsolved.

Shelburne's scheme required time. Answers from Governors could not be expected before March 1767. Long before that the ministry was in disarray. Chatham's visit to Bath became prolonged and, although he set off for London in February, an enforced stop in Marlborough meant that he was not in London until the first week in March. Moreover his illness, whatever it was, left him unable or unwilling to give his mind to business, and Grafton quite lacked the authority or courage to act without him. 'The Earl of Chatham', wrote the Earl of Buckinghamshire, 'is still at Bath, and consequently the King's administration has got the gout and hobbles terribly.'[24] In this situation Shelburne's authority, too, was undercut, for he depended entirely on Chatham for his position. The field was therefore left open for Conway, whose authority as Leader of the House of Commons was already suffering from the taunts of his erstwhile friends, and Townshend. Both opposed Chatham's East India policy; and Townshend, a long-standing supporter of taxing the colonists for the purpose of establishing a civil list there, was clearly unlikely to accept Shelburne's plans, even if they proved practicable. Moreover, as Chancellor of the Exchequer, he was faced with demands for a solution to the revenue problem, requests for a reduction in the National Debt, and pressure for an alleviation of the land tax burden. This situation was to affect American policy profoundly, but that policy was largely arrived at by accident, unnoticed. It was India which dominated the thoughts of administration and opposition alike, and American policy largely happened by default.

Not entirely by default, of course, for Charles Townshend had in 1753 made clear his belief in the need to raise a revenue by statute for the upkeep of civil government, and perhaps the army, in America. Therefore his intervention in American affairs cannot have been a surprise for Grafton. Nor can Townshend be blamed for offering his own plan when it became clear from the Governor's replies that Shelburne's hopes for the collection of quit rents were to be disappointed. However, Townshend's policy was not chiefly a response to Shelburne's failure. On 26 January Grenville moved an amendment to Barrington's resolution for supply for the upkeep of the army in America to the effect that it should be paid by the colonists of America and the West Indies. Townshend 'opposed the motion but with great civility – much approved the general idea of taxing America ... and that the notion of Internal Taxation and External Taxation [revenue duties] was perfect nonsense' (James Harris).[25] In this way Townshend ridiculed Chatham's own use of this – in truth illogical – distinction, and seemed to promise to raise a tax without offence, a fact which seems to have gone largely unnoted except by Shelburne, who informed Chatham on 1 February of a plan for a new board of customs in America 'and by a new regulation of the tea duty here and some other alterations, to provide a revenue of imports there'.[26] On 18 February Townshend again pointed out the absurdity of a distinction between internal and external taxation but argued that as Americans had themselves made such a distinction it was 'proper to be adopted in policy'. Finally he pledged the government to reduce the land tax from four shillings to three shillings in the pound on 27 February.

In none of this was Townshend acting in consultation with his cabinet colleagues; in fact he probably had more contact with opposition. Grafton wrote in his Memoirs in 1806 that 'no one of the ministry had authority sufficient to advise the dismissal of Mr Charles Townshend and nothing else could have stopped the measure, Lord Chatham's absence being in this instance, as well as others, much to be lamented'.

Chatham himself failed to persuade Lord North to take Townshend's place on 4 March, and, having made that supreme effort for his country, sank back into uncommunicative torpor from which not even his King could rouse him.

Although Townshend's policy of the Revenue Act was not accepted until May, when Shelburne finally admitted defeat in his own plans, he had begun working on it in March or even earlier. Parliamentary opinion ran strongly in Townshend's favour and his plans were public knowledge in April. It was assumed by many that the duties' main purpose would be to raise a revenue sufficient to cover the cut in the land tax; but this was not the case and never had been, though it certainly added to its popularity. His main aim was to impose a tax and establish a principle, the amount raised being very small. At a meeting with colonial agents 'The Chancellor of the Exchequer . . . declared . . . that although he did not in the least doubt the right of Parliament to tax the colonies internally and that he knew no distinction between internal and external laws . . . yet since the Americans were pleased to make that distinction he was willing to indulge them.'[27]

Grenville denounced Townshend's proposals as quite inadequate, as fiscally they were, but the purpose of Townshend's duties was political. He has been accused of mere cynical opportunism; while it is true that he was taking advantage of Franklin's assertion that the colonists had no objection to revenue duties (external taxation), he had long sought to assert Parliament's right to tax, and that was their chief purpose. Townshend was no fool, but as a revenue producing measure the Act of 1767 was a nonsense. It put duties on certain imports into the colonies such as glass, paint, and tea, of which only the last would produce a useful income. The system of importing tea into Britain, paying duty, collecting the duty back on re-export to the colonies, and repaying duty on arrival in America was clearly wasteful. But the use of monies collected for providing the beginnings of a civil list for Governors and other officials, the establishment of an American Board of Customs in Boston, and the authorisation of the issue of writs of assistance by superior colonial courts all pointed the real direction of Townshend's ideas.

It is remarkable at first sight that the Revenue Act should have been passed with so little comment either from 'Friends of America' within the ministry or opposition without. The Rockinghamites made no opposition; Grenville's assault concentrated on fiscal absurdities. The affairs of the East India Company rather than those of America filled the politicians' minds and it was unlikely that a measure that was supposed to be connected with a reduction in land tax would be opposed by any group or individual with pretensions to office. In addition, [declining goodwill towards the colonists and an almost universal belief in Parliament's right to tax, aided by confused thinking over external as opposed to internal taxation, made it unlikely that any serious opposition would surface to what was to become one of the most devastating blows to the relationship between Britain and her colonies.]

The ministry in the summer of 1767 survived largely because there was no alternative. In May, Conway, alone among ministers, opposed Townshend's three resolutions on America, condemning New York for disobeying the Mutiny Act and the inadequacy of New York's provisions and threatening to withhold assent to Acts of the New York legislature until the Act was complied with. He was mildly applauded by Rockingham but the Grenvillites and Bedfordites found Townshend altogether too generous to the colonists. Opposition therefore remained disunited, and not only over America, for Bute continued to exercise his influence over Rockingham's thoughts while Grenville and Bedford had long ceased to worry about him.

The campaign of attacks on the government demoralised Grafton and led the King, in effect deserted by Chatham, to look for ways of strengthening administration. Negotiations filled July. The Rockinghamites insisted on the prior dissolution of the ministry, the dismissal of any Butites and a complete ban on Grenville, though not Bedford. Thus political consistency involved persons but not policy. Grenville was prepared to let Bedford join Rockingham, but the King was not anxious to allow Rockingham to build a new ministry from scratch, based on party, and felt that Rockinghamite talent did not justify Rockinghamite pretensions. Bedford was not prepared to accept Rockingham's conceit either, and was more likely to benefit from a redistribution of offices in an existing administration than hope to secure a few places in a new ministry largely dictated by Rockingham. On this question, not on America or any issue of principle rather than party itself, the coalition of Rockingham and Bedford failed. The upshot of all of this was that the Bedfords entered the ministry alone in November. This had an important consequence for American policy, for it shifted the balance of the ministry away from conciliation to a harder line, though for reasons which should now be obvious, the effect of this can be exaggerated.

In September Townshend died and North accepted the office vacated. Chatham and Shelburne remained in the ministry for another year; but it was a very different ministry from the one which Pitt had formed in 1766 which now faced the consequences of Townshend's Revenue Act.

Even before the Revenue Act became law important events had taken place in the colonies. In 1766 in Massachusetts the popular party, led by Otis and Sam Adams, had secured control of the House of Representatives and infiltrated the Governor's council, and the issue of the quarrel with Britain was kept alive by the questions of compensation and indemnity. This pattern was repeated in other colonies which had, moreover, learned how vulnerable British government in the colonies was to a well-organised campaign of resistance. So the Townshend duties did not fall on unprepared ground. Nor did they alone fall on the colonists. Accompanying the Act was the creation under the Great Seal of four vice-admiralty districts and on 17 January the British troops in America began to be concentrated along the eastern seaboard.

An initial difficulty facing the colonists in resisting the

duties was the confusion existing over the issue of internal and external taxes. Franklin certainly accepted such a distinction; Lieutenant-Governor Hutchinson wrote that this distinction 'agrees with the opinion of most people here' (that is, in Massachusetts), and a pamphlet put out by the assembly of Connecticut had as its title *Reasons why the British Colonies shall not be charged with internal taxes*. Historians, mostly American, have argued that the colonists did not accept this distinction. Patrick Henry certainly never did. The confusion arises out of differentiation which must be made, but which usually was not, between customs impositions for the purpose of raising a revenue – for example a penny on a gallon of molasses – and impositions for inhibiting trade – for example, sixpence a gallon on foreign molasses. They are both customs dues and in that sense intended to raise a revenue; but one was meant to be paid – the other was not, and therefore was not a tax.

At first resistance to the duties was not universal because they were seen as regulatory and not fiscal; but John Dickinson's *Letters from a Farmer in Pennsylvania to the Inhabitants of the British Colonies*, published between December 1767 and February 1768, alerted the colonists to their danger and urged them to defend their rights 'peaceably, prudently, firmly, jointly'. Before the *Farmer's Letters* the Massachusetts assembly had denied Parliament's right to raise any revenue from the colonies and circulated other assemblies, and the Boston radicals and merchants, separately, had begun the non-consumption movement designed to unite the leading colonists in a peaceful form of resistance and once again rouse the support of British merchants. Redress, wrote Otis, 'is to be sought in a legal and constitutional way'. This movement, jealously managed by the merchants, steadily grew in effectiveness until by 1770, it had spread from Maine to Georgia, after which merchant opinion, satisfied by concessions from North, increasingly alarmed by radicalism, and afraid of violence, left the radicals to continue the struggle alone against what was then the sole remaining Townshend duty, that on tea. But resistance also took the form of circular letters between assemblies' committees of correspondence, the revival by the radicals of the Sons of Liberty which proliferated throughout the colonies in 1769–70, and organised boycotts and social ostracism. These committees and the organisation of the Sons of Liberty were to continue after 1770, and by that year they had accomplished a permanent network of people and institutions capable of running an alternative government.

Despite every effort mob activity was not avoided. After the navy's seizure of radical John Hancock's ship *Liberty* for smuggling in June 1768, a Boston mob forced customs officers to take refuge on board HMS *Romney*. Four regiments were sent to Boston and disembarked on 1 October. Order was restored; but royal government functioned only in the interstices of that provided by merchant organisations and Sons of Liberty.

The infamous duties had a short life. Although Viscount Hillsborough, the first Secretary of State for the newly created Colonial Department, urged a reform of the Massachusetts charter to modify the Governor's council and a law by which any questioning of the right of Parliament to tax the colonies would lead to the automatic cancelling of the charter, the Grafton administration chose to ignore the advice from one of Halifax's friends, and his other advice – to cancel the Townshend duties, albeit on fiscal rather than constitutional grounds – was a concession to America which became politically dangerous when colonists so vehemently denied parliamentary sovereignty.

In fact, Grafton's ministry oscillated between threats to assert supremacy and suggestions of a less forceful approach, perhaps inevitably so in a ministry composed of hawks and doves. In the summer of 1768 Hillsborough moved towards a show of force, dispatching two regiments to the colonies from Ireland and urging his colleagues to follow General Gage's advice from Boston to take decisive action. At the same time Camden, a Pittite, urged that it was 'inexpedient to tax the colonies' and that 'there is nothing I dread so much as a war with America'.[28]

Such divisions in cabinet and George III's own dislike of altering charters – 'at all times an odious measure' – made it unlikely that decisive action of the kind demanded by Hillsborough and Gage would be taken, and eventually brought about a compromise in the spring of 1769 over what to do about the Townshend duties. Complete surrender was deemed likely to lead to pressure from the colonies for the repeal of the Navigation Acts and would have been very unpopular in cabinet and Parliament, and so the repeal of all but Townshend's duty on tea to uphold the principle of sovereignty was eventually agreed upon, the abolition of the other duties being defended on the basis of sound commercial sense. The repeal was carried out by North's administration in March 1770, two months after Grafton's resignation.

There is no doubt that the Townshend duties and their aftermath mark an important turning point in the American crisis. That politicians in Britain could now speak of the need for military action, the alteration of charters and the need to arrange trials of individuals for treason in special British courts, proved beyond doubt that many believed that the whole future of the Empire was at stake. In a letter to Rockingham in December 1768, following news of the Massachusetts assembly's circular letter which denounced all forms of parliamentary taxation and set Governor Bernard at defiance, Dowdeswell spelled out the stark choice facing Britain if other cities followed Boston's rebellious example. If Britain gave up the principle of parliamentary sovereignty she was giving up more than a means of producing a revenue; if she insisted on her rights she faced the likelihood of war with her colonies, who would be aided and abetted by her traditional enemies, France and Spain. Either way, the loss of her colonies seemed likely. Camden said that the assertion of right would be 'fatal to Great Britain, if she miscarries: unprofitable if she succeeds'.[29] The point, of course, was that now elements on both sides seemed determined to stand on principle, and even if such a stand was, for the moment, postponed, the bedrock of principle had been reached. The colonies denied parliamentary supremacy;

Parliament was obliged to defend it.

Luckily Grafton's administration was not united and did not proceed to confrontation. Although the American issue had now assumed an importance in British political thinking far beyond any previous point, it was still only one of the issues driving Grafton to distraction. The Middlesex election and its aftermath in the petitioning movement was a more immediate difficulty which brought together Chathamites, Grenvillites and Rockinghamites into a common cause, which America never could. To America John Wilkes, the radical demagogue, was a hero; to the politicians, and even to many in the Society of Supporters of the Bill of Rights, he was a squalid nuisance, but he raised an important constitutional issue as well as the emotive banner of 'Liberty'. The apparent success of the movement, when a quarter of the electorate petitioned Parliament, probably misled many colonists into thinking that there was a more effective and vocal backing for their cause in Britain than was the case. In fact the petitions very largely depended on the willingness of grandees to back them and are a poor guide to popular opinion. American agents believed that the Wilkes issue at least predisposed the administration to concession.

In February 1770 the Boston massacre signalled that the troubles were not over, but by then, disheartened by the death of Charles Yorke, the bitter assaults of Junius, the anonymous author of the famous *Letters*, and the wounding oratory of a revived Chatham, Grafton had resigned.

The chronology of events between 1760 and 1770 and the entrenched positions which seemed to have been taken up on both sides by the end of the decade might suggest that after the Stamp Act conflict was inevitable, and certainly Burke feared that the emphasis on rights would lead to conflict. But Benjamin Franklin in 1769 reported of the administration's view of the Townshend duties, 'they cannot bear the denial of the right of Parliament to make them, tho' they acknowledge they ought not to have been made'.[30] It was this combination of a belief in parliamentary supremacy with an unwillingness to stir up colonial resentment, from whatever motives, which characterised the attitudes of most politicians to the colonial question.

As to the general belief in the sovereignty of Parliament and its *right* to tax the colonies in this period, there can be no doubt. In 1765 Thomas Whately, MP for Ludgershall and Secretary to the Treasury, had stated that the Stamp Bill's purpose was to establish 'the right of Parliament to levy an internal tax upon the colonies'. There were no doubts about an *external* tax which was seen simply as a revenue duty with which colonials were as familiar as the British, and only later would the distinction be clearly made by the colonists between a revenue duty as a tax and an imposition as a means of regulating trade, a distinction which anyway makes more sense in theory than it does in practice. (As William Knox, agent for Georgia, satirically pointed out in *The Controversy between Great Britain and her Colonies Reviewed* (1769), 'The right of Parliament to charge foreign molasses with a duty of six-pence was unquestionable; but for Parliament to reduce the six-pence to three-pence is a violent usurpation of unconstitutional authority.')

The right of Parliament to levy an internal tax was unequivocally stated by the Rockingham Whigs in the Declaratory Act, where Parliament, it is affirmed, 'had, hath and of right ought to have full power and validity to bind the colonies and people of America in all cases whatsoever', thus upholding the principle behind the Grenville Stamp Act. Only Pitt and one or two of his allies, such as Beckford, demurred. On 16 January 1765 the Great Commoner Pitt declared that Parliament had 'no right to levy an internal tax on America' though he too asserted Parliament's sovereignty in other matters and supported the idea of a right of external taxation. But the majority opinion, and certainly the view of most independents, was clearly contrary to this assertion.

The ease with which the Stamp Act was passed and the equally limited opposition against which the Townshend duties were passed underlines the fact that most politicians accepted the right to tax without question and partly explains the failure of opposition in this period. In 1765–6, during the campaign for the repeal of the Stamp Act, the Rocking-hamites emphasised the commercial damage supposedly done by the Act and steered discussion in Parliament away from constitutional issues. It is also worth noting that among initial Rockinghamite reactions to America's resistance to the Stamp Act Conway urged 'timely Exertion of Force' and although Rockingham would not go so far he planned 'to execute [the Act] by fair means . . .'

The unanimity of view helps to explain some of the apparent contradictions and confusions in the British response to American affairs. The Rockinghamite American Duties Act, by lowering the duty on foreign molasses entering the colonies to one penny, effectively taxed the colonists as surely as Grenville's Sugar Act which this measure now repealed. Rockinghamite indifference to the passing of Townshend's duties emphasises the point.

It often seems strange to students of the period that differences over America should not have prevented factions from joining in coalition or at least from discussing such conjunctions. But perhaps one reason why Bedford and Rockingham could discuss a union in 1767, or why men such as the Bedfordites and Hillsborough could join Grafton's administration is that there was no difference of *principle* between them on the American issue and that practical application of principles would always be open to modification by the exigencies of the moment or by the natural tendencies of politicians to compromise.

'Every man in England', wrote Benjamin Franklin in 1767, 'seems to consider himself as a piece of sovereign over America, seems to jostle into the throne with the King and talks of *our* subjects in the colonies.' The idea of sovereignty over the colonies was thus buoyed up with the pride of possession, hardly surprising after the Seven Years' War, and that pride of possession was itself reinforced by the fear of France. It is not to be wondered at that in the age of Pitt the Elder and expansionist activity by all major powers the need to maintain possession of the colonies in order to preserve national greatness was seen as self-evident and paramount. All politicians shared this view. Parliamentary sovereignty was reinforced by nationalism and the need for national survival. It is not amazing that it was so universally supported.

But, as has already been suggested, the assertion of supremacy had always so far been tempered by other considerations. Grenville himself had revealed one of these considerations in presenting his plans for the Stamp Act. We have already seen how a belief in the rightness of representative institutions and a fear of coercing them had been a major factor inhibiting British controls on the growth of colonial legislative independence in the reigns of George III's immediate predecessors. Grenville felt obliged in his presentation of the Bill to go to the heart of the matter; whether Parliament could levy an *internal* tax despite 'the general right of mankind not to be taxed but by their own representative', a right which he himself asserted. He made use of the idea of virtual representation, the indirect representation of property interests. Just as 'the Parliament of Great Britain virtually represents the whole kingdom, not actually the great trading towns' whose interests were looked after by the existence of some parliamentary boroughs sharing the same interests, so the colonies were represented by MPs whose interests coincided with those of the colonies. James Otis made short shrift of the idea but it was acceptable to most in Britain before the nineteenth century. Nonetheless, what is significant here is Grenville's care to argue that he was not offending colonial representative institutions. He also took care publicly, if perhaps cynically, to offer the colonial assemblies the chance to produce an alternative scheme of self-taxation. Before 1774 no attempt was made to interfere with colonial parliamentary institutions, the King in 1768 clearly vetoing any alteration in Massachusetts' charter. Besides, in the eighteenth century, charter rights, customs sanctified by long use, and property rights were rarely challenged, for society was fundamentally traditional in its outlook and breaches in prescriptive rights and liberties would have been revolutionary and justifiable only by revolution.

A reluctance to use force is also a clear feature of the politicians' attitude to the colonies. A major consideration was the size of the army. In 1768 the King would not permit Hillsborough to send more troops to Boston because of the need to keep sufficient troops in Britain in the event of civil disturbance, which between 1765 and 1770 was distinctly possible. Equally, however, there was the feeling that the use of the army should always be a last resort. Cromwell and James II were still alive in the minds of eighteenth-century politicians. Moreover it was so often the case that the presence of troops could provoke disorder or give an excuse for it, as with the Boston and the St George's Fields Massacres. The peaceful disembarkation of the two regiments in Boston was greeted by the government in Westminster with relief. The troops themselves were withdrawn from the town after 1770; the last thing they wanted was for a war to break out.

Conciliation and circumspection is the chief feature of Westminster's response to the colonists' complaints, always with the proviso that the *right* to tax and legislate in all matters be maintained. The Stamp Act was repealed; the Sugar Act was repealed, the Townshend duties all but. No doubt the ministers were influenced by the problem of enforcement. In 1765 Newcastle had said that he did not see how the colonists could be coerced. The army in America until after 1768 was on the frontier, not the seaboard. There was no rapid deployment of force ready to be dispatched even if it had been thought desirable. The Governors depended in their exercise of power on the support of the colonial oligarchy. The Rockinghamites certainly decided very quickly that enforcement was impossible.

But there were other considerations too. The care for the rights of legislatures and fear of anything which might strengthen the executive certainly influenced politicians. The Rockinghamites were heirs to that tradition of 'salutary neglect' pursued by the Old Corps of Whigs in George II's reign and Pitt's followers, too, saw themselves as 'Friends of America', opposed to any policy which seemed punitive. There were politicians such as Hillsborough, Charles Townshend, and the supporters of Bedford and Grenville who felt that the assertion of the right to internal tax must be material and not just declaratory but they were not a majority. In Grafton's administration almost every suggestion made by Hillsborough for the punishment of Massachusetts was blocked by Grafton, Conway, Camden and the King, and any attempt to extend coercion to another colony, such as Virginia or New York, was firmly resisted. The idea of an expanded Quartering Act for the colonies was thus rejected and the government satisfied itself with a re-enactment of the existing statute.

The tendency to conciliate and avoid conflict was equally present in the colonies, helping to give rise to that feeling among politicians in Britain that the removal of a few hothead radicals would put all to rights. It is true that the Americans' denial of Parliament's right to tax at all was potentially destructive of the Empire and equally true that the colonists saw in the Middlesex election crisis further evidence of the decline of liberty in Britain and of the tyrannical tendencies not just of a few isolated politicians but of a whole political class, a feeling heightened by the fortuitous proximity of the 'massacres' at Boston and St George's Fields. But the Boston affair's aftermath underlines the fact that few in America wished to push principle as far as a breach. The efforts made by leading Whigs in Boston to provide for the defence of the soldiers arraigned for the shootings is testimony to this.

In 1766, on hearing of the repeal of the Stamp Act, the vast majority of those who had led the opposition rejoiced and, ignoring the evidence of the Declaratory Act, took Parliament's actions in good faith. The Sons of Liberty were largely disbanded. In 1769 and 1770 the alacrity with which the merchant community abandoned non-consumption agreements on the promised repeal of the Townshend duties is evidence of their financial losses which they must have feared would grow enormously in the event of any prolonged conflict or, worse, permanent divorce from the British Empire. Disappointment at the almost total absence of support from the commercial community of Britain and inter-colonial rivalry also played their part in the collapse of the movement. But it needs to be emphasised that the merchants' campaign against the duties was quite separate from that of the Sons of Liberty and other radical organisations. Sam Adams in 1770 described himself and the Boston Sons of Liberty as 'not connected, but as an Auxiliary in their Non-Importation Agreement'.[31] Therefore, although the ability of the non-importers and their allies to establish a virtual alternative government in the colonies and the continuation of much of that organisation after 1770 were potentially revolutionary, leading colonists were still reluctant to push their claims to a logical conclusion. Sam Adams and his associates vainly pointed out in 1770 that Parliament had not conceded the point of right; he kept his committees of correspondence and Sons of Liberty in operation and looked for further means of creating dissension, but merchants and other leading members of colonial society still feared men like Adams as much as they feared Parliament. The democratic principles stressed by radicals in their formulation of arguments against Britain and the increasingly successful inroads made into colonial legislatures were a threat to oligarchic control throughout the colonies. It was, after all, not for nothing that 100 000 Loyalist colonists emigrated to Canada and Britain at the end of the War of Independence. Only when the fear of what might happen if the radicals were given their head was outweighed by what Britain was doing to threaten the colonists would men like John Adams finally decide that independence was inevitable and desirable. Meanwhile, although firebells were ringing in the night, enough men on both sides of the Atlantic still wanted to prevent the clash of opposite principles turning to armed conflict.

From this distance and with the gift of hindsight it would

seem obvious that the problem of America must have weighed heavily on the politicians – administration and opposition – in this period, and of course it began to loom larger as the first decade of George III's reign progressed, but it would be wrong to assume that they were obsessed with it.

America played very little part in the rise or fall of ministries at this time. George Grenville's administration saw no quarrel between King and ministers on America.[32] The King rarely interfered with matters of policy, accepting as he did the consequences of the idea of ministerial responsibility. He wholeheartedly, even stubbornly, defended parliamentary sovereignty and after Grenville's fall urged his new ministers to modify rather than repeal the Stamp Act, though the Act itself hardly features at all in the correspondence between Grenville and his sovereign.

Grenville fell because George III finally found politicians willing to replace him, when the Newcastle–Rockingham faction agreed by a narrow margin to provide the King with a ministry, even without Pitt. George III's disgust at his treatment by the ministry had made it likely that he would rid himself of Grenville and he had made several attempts. It was Grenville's excessive interference in what the King saw as his personal patronage and the extraordinary ill-will generated by the Regency Act which finally provoked the breach. Personal antipathy not America ended Grenville's career in government.

Prerogative brought the Rockinghamites to power. There were no stipulations as to policy but it soon became clear that leading elements in the formulation of Rockinghamite policy were the fear of Bute and the desire to discredit Grenville. Hence the repeal of the Cider Excise, the abolition of General Warrants and, in part, the repeal of the Stamp Act.

The end of Rockingham's ministry is more intimately bound up with America but America was one of the occasions of the quarrel between King and ministers, not its cause. The Rockinghamites themselves, never keen to see the beam in their own eye, blamed all on the malign influence of

Bute. Obsessed by fear of Bute, a desire to undermine Grenville's reputation and the attitude to itself of Pitt, the ministry, after Cumberland's death, distanced itself from Bute and from Grenville's legislation. The repeal of the Stamp Act and the passage of the Declaratory Act created opportunities for Grenville and disgruntled Butites, or King's Friends as they are often misleadingly known, to make trouble.

The King's Friends, dissatisfied by the predictable failure of Rockingham to promote their interests, also in general preferred modification to repeal of the Stamp Act, a view shared by George III. But the King refused Lord Harcourt's advice to make this view public, saying 'he would never influence people in their parliamentary opinions that he had promised to support his ministers.'[33] Unfortunately the King's attempt in January 1766 to set up a new ministry created suspicion of royal intentions in the ministry while the King himself became irritated by the ministry's efforts to secure an alliance with Pitt, on one occasion at least in flat contradiction to his orders.

Dissatisfaction among the King's Friends was evident in February when some of their number, a 'Flying Squadron', contributed to two minor defeats for the administration, one being on the fourth resolution for the Declaratory Bill in the Lords, where Bute and the King's brother, the Duke of York, were part of the majority.

The King publicly reiterated his support for his administration's policy, but he did not, as he had promised in July 1765, dismiss rebellious Butites. This incident contributed to the Whig myth of an unconstitutional monarch using secret influence to unseat his government. 'The Strange Affair' added to the growing discontent. In a private conversation with Lord Strange on 10 February the King stated his preference for modification rather than repeal. Strange, a friend of Grenville's, made public this inopportunely expressed opinion which led to an uncomfortable interview with Rockingham.

America therefore provided occasion but not source for

the ill-will which helped to end this ministry. Rockinghamite suspicion of Bute and the King's supposed continued support for him were the real cause of the antagonism. But the fall of the ministry owed a great deal to ministerial incompetence and the failure to secure Pitt which led to Grafton's resignation. The Hon. John Yorke, a junior member of the administration, described it as '. . . a Vessel without officers and a crew undisciplin'd . . . what a Medley of Characters and Connections'[34] an interesting opinion given Burke's later strictures on Chatham's ministry, and the Rockinghamites' own party pretensions.

Newcastle was appalled by the insistence on replacing Grafton with Richmond, a nobleman known to be personally offensive to the King. The ill-management of the Duke of Cumberland's civil list also gave offence while the King could never understand the pursuit of Pitt when the ministry could be strengthened from the proven talents of those gentlemen known as Butites but better described, perhaps, as 'friends to good government'.

America then did no more than provide part of the battleground on which skirmishes between King and ministers took place. Nor did it create the divisions within the Rockinghamites, far yet from being a party, which led to resignations and royal displeasure. On America royal support was unwavering, if on occasion ineptly managed.

Pitt's emergence as leader of a reconstituted ministry in 1766 might have been expected to have been influenced by America. His opposition to internal taxation and to the Declaratory Act had caused Americans to make a hero of him and to raise statues in his honour. But Pitt became leading minister because the old ministry was falling apart, and because the King realised that he could call on Pitt without having to put up with the dreaded Grenvillites. It was not the least of Pitt's virtues too that he abhorred party and connection just as much as did his sovereign. He would stand as the enemy of all parties 'like a primeval parent, naked because innocent; naked not ashamed'.[35]

The appointment of Shelburne to the Southern Secretaryship suggested new vigour in colonial affairs, though after New York's misbehaviour over the Mutiny Act, Chatham washed his hands of the colonists. The Declaratory Act remained on the statute book, Shelburne's plans collapsed, and Townshend went ahead, largely independently. Chatham's lengthy illness and sulk allowed an American policy to be promoted by others.

It is significant that during negotiations between opposition groups in 1767 the cause of the collapse of plans for a joint opposition or ministry between Bedford and Rockingham was very little concerned with America. Although Rockingham would have nothing to do with Grenville and the Stamp Act might have been an element in this, it was more Grenville's ability and following, to say nothing of his personality, which put off the Rockinghamites. Bedford's support for the Stamp Act was unquestioned and yet this was no source of difficulty. Far more important in preventing unity were disputes over the future of Conway, the disposition of offices and the Rockinghamite insistence on being treated as a superior connection or party, which prevented fusion. Bedford entered a ministry still ostensibly led by the bitter opponent of the Stamp Act and Declaratory Act and containing many of those who had repealed the former. This action was not seen as odd, nor did it upset relations with Grenville.

America was an issue in politics but it had little influence on the rise and fall of ministers; it figured only in a minor way in discussions between potential coalition partners. Partly this is because, as we have seen, politicians shared basic assumptions about the purpose of the colonies and the rights of Parliament. Partly it is a result of a lack of any real ideological divisions in a small ruling élite which saw issues as relatively minor elements in politics, matters which could be sorted out pragmatically; and such an attitude was reinforced by the lack of any hard and fast concept of cabinet responsibility. The career of Townshend should alert us to that fact and Northington, Lord Chancellor in Rockingham's ministry, saw himself primarily as the King's man and was instrumental in the negotiations which ended that administration. Conway, in Chatham's administration, maintained a loyalty to Rockingham. Government was still largely departmental.

Finally it needs to be repeated that for much of the time India and Wilkes, rather than America, dominated the political scene. Chatham hardly spent any of his time as leader of the ministry engaged on America. Foreign policy – the doomed attempt to secure an alliance with Prussia; together with India, and the determination to assert the Crown's rights to the new territories conquered by the East India Company – dominated the first months of his ministry. India was a commanding issue because the vast acquisitions made by the Company, far beyond its capacity to control, nonetheless encouraged expectations of huge profits, led to speculation in shares, and provided fruitful ground for party patronage.[36] India rather than America was the jewel in the Crown. The East India interest was much closer to home and much more powerfully organised in Parliament, and the value of India as a colony was seen to be even greater than that of other colonies, while crises of management kept the Company's affairs in the limelight.

The potential for social disturbance created by Wilkes in 1763 but especially in 1768–9 while London was beset by the consequences of a depression, an influx of people from the countryside and strikes, needs hardly be emphasised. Equally, Wilkes provided an issue which could unite opposition in the petitioning movement of 1769 and 1770.

It is therefore not surprising that American issues were not always at the forefront of politics as we might imagine, from what followed, they should have been. This in turn may help us to understand why so little opposition to the American policy of successive governments was forthcoming.

Opposition to American policy was minimal throughout the 1760s. The answer lies to some extent in the nature of eighteenth-century government. A Treasury minister, apparently favoured by the King, could almost always secure a majority in the House of Commons, particularly, if like

Grenville or North, he proved to be a sound guardian of the country's fiscal and economic strength. In the House of Lords the Court was unchallengeably supreme and its influence in the Commons through closed boroughs and family ties was very potent. Patronage, the support of MPs whose patrons or relations in the Lords were administration men, and the feeling, especially strong among independent MPs, that the King's chosen minister ought to be upheld, guaranteed a minister the House's confidence in all but the most abnormal circumstances. Besides this, it must never be forgotten that the Stamp Act and Townshend's duties were popular with landed classes seeking relief from the high taxes needed to service a huge National Debt and affronted by colonial pretensions.

The governing élite of the United Kingdoms was narrow; just how narrow has been demonstrated in several recent studies.[37] That élite, with very few exceptions, believed in the sovereignty of Parliament, agreed that the colonies existed to serve the mother country, and were convinced that loss of power over the colonies would mean defeat by France, a view shared by foreign powers. It was little influenced by 'public opinion', whatever that might mean in the eighteenth century. The opinion which mattered was that of the political nation and although the élite used the press, it was not influenced by it.[38] Even if we knew what the public at large felt about America, and the mass of Englishmen were felt to be jingoists, that knowledge would be irrelevant.

Parliamentary opposition to the passage of the Stamp Act was virtually non-existent. The followers of Rockingham and Newcastle were more concerned with General Warrants and their relationship with Pitt. Only William Beckford, the former Jacobite and now a radical MP for the City, and Pitt's political agent there, as well as part of the West Indies interest, opposed the Act consistently from its first mooting to its first reading. Beckford denied the right of internal taxation, though not of external, as in the Sugar Act. He was seconded in his opposition to the Stamp Act by Colonel Barré, a recent convert to Pitt, but Barré did not deny

Parliament's *right* to levy the tax, only the wisdom of doing so. Supported only by Richard Jackson, agent for Connecticut, Massachusetts and Pennsylvania, Thomas Townshend and Sir William Meredith, a 'convert from Jacobitism' and now a follower of Rockingham, these men could do little. Pitt himself probably shared Beckford's opposition to an internal tax but was too ill, too distracted or too bored to make his views known.

More opposition might have been expected from the West Indies interest, for after all the constitutional implications of the Stamp Act were the same for Jamaica as for Virginia. But the interest in the House of Commons, though numbering about twenty, muted any potential resistance to the measure, for the position of planters in an overwhelmingly black society did not admit of serious quarrels with Britain, while the Sugar Act had pleased the West Indies planters greatly.

The agents for North American colonies proved to be 'a rope of sand'. There were eighteen colonial agents during the passage of the Stamp Act, some acting for more than one colony, some sharing the agency for another. Handicapped by distance, by instructions often offensive to Parliament or too rigid, they did not act in unison. Many were not in a position to be forceful opponents; and as few were, like Richard Jackson, MPs, they had to rely on lobbying. Among those who were MPs dependence on Grenville by John Sargent, MP for Looe and an agent for New York, perhaps limited his effectiveness, though similar connections did not inhibit Richard Jackson or Charles Garth (Devizes). Only one American, John Huske, MP for Maldon, sat in the House in this period and he was probably abroad during the passage of the bill. Merchants trading with America were also ill-represented – only about a dozen led by Sir William Baker whose opposition to Grenville was total on every issue. On the Stamp Act he 'rambled . . . and acts the patriot, this rather awkwardly' (Harris).

It cannot therefore surprise us to find that Townshend's duties met with little opposition. Despite the obvious likelihood of a hostile colonial response in the atmosphere of heightened awareness, consequent on the Stamp Act crisis, little comment was forthcoming from 'Friends of America' in the ministry or outside it. The Rockinghamites said nothing as a party about Townshend's proposals, despite their well-advertised reputation for consistency and the Chancellor of the Exchequer's blatant taunting of the agents in his ridicule of the concept of a difference of principle between internal and external impositions. Politicians' minds were concentrated on India rather than America, and opposition's energies on winning short-term skirmishes with the ministry over, for example, land tax, and on the possibility of ministerial changes. It is also sad but true that few people, least of all other politicians, listen to what politicians actually say. More to the point politicians were united on Parliament's right to tax, and the distinction between internal and external taxation was one which seemed obviously reasonable. After all, it inhibited American resistance to Townshend's duties until Dickinson provided the distinction between a levy as a means of directing or inhibiting trade and a levy as a means of raising a revenue. Given that the colonists never denied the right of Parliament to manage the trade of the Empire, the idea of raising a revenue through impositions small enough to be paid and likely to prevent smuggling was bound to be attractive to Parliament, particularly if associated with a reduction in land tax. The Sugar Act had been accepted by the colonists, the Rockinghamites had passed their American Duties Act which had taxed the colonies through customs impositions, so it would now be merely wilful, or suggestive of a revolutionary impulse, if the colonists resisted the duty. Neither the colonial agents nor the West Indies interest, who had stood to benefit from the Sugar Act, were in a position to offer any coherent opposition to Townshend.

'A repeated opposition from that side of the water upon a principle directed against all duties for revenue must be met. It must either be admitted or resisted', wrote Dowdeswell to his party leader Rockingham. In 1767 Franklin noted that 'Every man in England seems to consider himself as a piece of sovereign over America.' Given the unanimity of opinion among British politicians and the revolutionary implications of *The Farmer's Letters*, it is hardly surprising if disputes over colonial policy featured little in discussions among politicians during the search for a stable ministry between 1767 and 1770. It is more extraordinary perhaps that on both sides there still remained such a strong desire to avoid a clash of principles from which neither could back down.

3

LORD NORTH AND THE LOSS OF THE AMERICAN COLONIES 1770–83

'The die is cast'

Lord North was one of the most able peacetime Prime Ministers of the eighteenth century. Although at first his ministry was not expected to last, it had many assets. North himself was a highly competent administrator and manager of finances. As Colonel Barré, a Shelburnite opponent, said in 1774: 'It is looked upon not only as unfashionable, but foolish to get up and dispute what is in the Budget'. His use of lotteries and reduction of the National Debt pleased the country gentlemen and the financiers alike and enabled him to reduce interest on loan stock. His career had seen him holding office under every administration except that of Rockingham since 1759, and he had therefore won himself no great political enemies. Lord Dartmouth, North's step-brother and a Rockinghamite, secured him a degree of toleration initially at least, even in that self-important party. His good humour in debate, his assiduous attendance in the House and his frequent speeches made few enemies, even among his political opponents, and won him great affection in the House of whose interests he was seen as champion. The acquisition of the Grenvillites under the Earl of Suffolk and the return of Grafton to office in 1771, in addition to the effects on the Bedfordites of Bedford's retirement and the Falkland Islands dispute in which an attempt to challenge North's authority had been defeated, made him undisputed head of a broadly-based administration. Above all he had the unwavering support of the King, given visible proof in the award of the Garter, and less visible testimony in the gift of the Rangership of Bushey Park and royal help for his beleagured finances. King, Treasury and Commons were once again united in one man and faction had declined. Opposition was left to Chathamites and Rockinghamites and that opposition was weak and divided.

On America North had generally been in favour of moderation but he had left office in 1765 with Grenville and opposed Stamp Act Repeal. In 1770 he carried out the policy of repealing all of Townshend's duties but that on tea, and he left that specifically as an earnest of Parliament's determination to uphold its authority. His ministry after 1771 contained Grenvillites and Bedfordites committed in principle and by past policy to taxing the colonies. Lord North's was an administration of individuals not of party discipline or strong leadership. He believed in departmental rather than cabinet responsibility. This, though a telling burden on government during the war, was usual rather than unique in the period and in itself did not create the difficulties the ministers had in dealing with America.

Although on the surface relations between Parliament and the colonies seemed to have reached some sort of equilibrium at the time of Grafton's fall, appearances were deceptive. The reality was that the line established by the colonists and that maintained by Parliament were quite incompatible and seen as *ne plus ultra* lines by both. The Boston Massacre of 1770 gave a new twist to American suspicions of British intentions. American radicals did not let up in their efforts to inflame feelings. The network of committees of correspondence proliferated, not merely between, but within, colonies. The attack on a customs vessel in the Delaware river in 1771 was followed by a more serious incident in 1772, in which

HMS *Gaspée*, a revenue vessel, was boarded and destroyed. Although the guilty men were prominent citizens of Providence, Rhode Island, no prosecution could ever be brought. The Virginia House of Burgesses' reference, in 1773, to Great Britain as 'a foreign power' was hardly likely to calm British suspicions. The Speaker of the Massachusetts House of Representatives in 1773 wrote in reply to the Virginia committee of correspondence 'those who are aimed to enslave us . . . have ever been united in their Councils and their Conduct'.[1] In fact, of course, British policy until now had been largely unco-ordinated, reacting to events, and certainly not committed to any policy of 'enslavement'. But the threat of an American political union of opposition through committees of correspondence and British fears for its colonial power were bound to change this situation. The inflammatory 1773 addresses of the Massachusetts assembly and council denouncing British supremacy were, said Secretary Dartmouth, 'replete with doctrines of the most dangerous nature'.[2] The cabinet met to discuss Massachusetts' behaviour and advised the King that it was time to support Parliament's rights. But as it was late in the session and the East India Bill was taking up Parliament's time, it was decided to wait until a more opportune time.

The quarrel which erupted between Governor Thomas Hutchinson and the Massachusetts legislature when letters between Hutchinson and his deputy, Andrew Oliver, were published and maliciously misrepresented as evidence of a conspiracy against colonial liberties, did little to increase respect in Westminster for the colonial radicals or for Benjamin Franklin who was deeply involved. But the incident did not create the desire in Westminster to bring Boston to heel, though it did lead to the replacement of Hutchinson by Gage in 1774. What it and the more spectacular Boston Tea Party did do was to convince North's administration that it would be possible to isolate the Bostonians from the rest of the colonists and call up the loyalism which was deemed to lie in the hearts of the majority of Americans.

Once again India rather than America had exercised the

politicians in the early years of North's administration. Out of this concern had emerged the East India Company Regulating Act of 1773 by which the government came to exert a measure of political control over the Company's affairs in India and provide financial help. One such concession was to free the Company's tea from duties on re-export and to allow it to export tea to America through its own agents. In attempting to save the Company and avoid too much opposition North succeeded in upsetting the colonists. The Company's export of tea to America, through its own rather than American merchants, once again offended powerful American commercial interests, while radicals feared that the tea would be cheaper as a consequence of direct selling by the Company and would be bought by colonists, thus establishing a revenue as a result of more tea being consumed, all of it paying Townshend's threepenny duty. Lord North denied that the policy was cynically designed to do what the radicals feared. It is clear that the finances of the East India Company were his chief concern and that a step in the direction of the complete remission of import duties on tea entering Britain had already been made in 1772, which must have made tea already cheaper in America before the changes of 1773 and against which the colonies had made no protest. Nevertheless it is also probable that the government had refused the Company's request to abandon the threepence Townshend duty in return for the Company paying sixpence export duty on the tea leaving Britain for America, and while it is possible that North did not see any new principle in the arrangements of 1773, it is equally possible, in the light of the government's attitude to the colonists in 1773, that the administration had a hope of insinuating taxation on the colonists.

Opposition among parliamentary enemies of North's administration to the East India Regulating Bill was loud but ineffective in its concentration on the dangers of increased royal patronage and the threat to the balance of the Constitution. To the scheme to help the Company to sell its tea in America, however, the Rockinghamites offered little opposition and forecast no resistance. Opposition in America was of an altogether more effective kind. The Regulating Act reunited merchants and radicals in a common cause. In November the commissioners of a Boston customs house and five Company agents were driven to take refuge in Castle William. A month later the famous 'Tea Party' took place, though Boston was not the only city which refused to take the tea. Once again royal authority in the colonies was rendered powerless.

The Tea Party in its successful appeal to violence made it difficult for either side to draw back from confrontation. No administration in London could ignore so criminal an act, and Boston could not now withdraw from the stand it had taken. A flagrant assault on parliamentary and imperial authority, while not rendering conciliation impossible, did severely weaken the North administration's room to man-oeuvre, without concessions which might alter the whole nature of the Empire. It was radical policy to drive the government to extremes; the policy succeeded not because of any united and aggressive response on the part of the ministers, far from it, but because in such a situation where the colonists were making the running and the ministers were reacting to events not controlling them, where a desire to create conflict was met by a desire to avoid it, and where the administration's need to preserve Parliament's rights could not be bargained away, a drift to extremes was almost inevitable.

News of the activities of the men of Boston reached London on 27 January, two days before the privy council was already due to discuss the dispute between Governor Hutchinson and the Massachusetts assembly which had petitioned for his removal. Both affairs strengthened the feeling for strong action. The petition was rejected and the cabinet subsequently agreed to lay relevant papers before Parliament to take steps 'to secure the dependence of the Colonies on the Mother Country'.[3] It is clear, however, that even at this stage draconian measures would, it was hoped, be avoided. This was not because of any division between moderates and hard-liners, a division which is as irrelevant to this ministry as it was to all the others. Chatham's ministry had been 'Friends of America' but had passed the Townshend duties and tried to enforce the Mutiny Act: Grafton's ministry was dominated, it is said, by enemies to colonial pretensions, but decided to repeal all but one of the duties. The politicians reacted to events with the predispositions of Englishmen, Whigs and responsible ministers; but they also acted circumspectly, with an eye to maintaining peace and stability if they could. They were not firebrands; they did not enjoy conflagrations and they were as aware as Dowdeswell of the possible consequences of a civil war within the Empire. They tried to move circumspectly.

The cabinet decided in February to remove the government and assembly of Massachusetts from Boston, to consult the law officers as to whether treason had been spoken and if so what punishments to offer and to suspend Boston's privileges as a port. Originally it was hoped to do this by 'the sole authority of the Crown', wrote Dartmouth; but this proved impossible and therefore the matter had to be laid before Parliament for legislative redress. In the view of Bernard Donoghue this made the government policy 'more general in the application and more vindictive'.[4] The punishment of individuals by executive action would, in Dartmouth's view, have kept within the law and created less resentment; but now new laws had to be made. It is doubtful whether proceeding against individuals would have provoked much less resentment in Boston or its captive assembly; but the use of statute did help to turn a quarrel with the Massachusetts seaboard towns into a quarrel with all America.

The government's initial tactic of avoiding a constitutional struggle by not involving Parliament, but proceeding by executive action using existing laws, was abandoned because the law officers, Thurlow and Wedderburn, came to the conclusion that such a move was insufficiently legal. The consequence was the Intolerable Acts, as they have come to be known. These went through Parliament with remarkable speed and with unanimity of purpose in the cabinet, even from Lord Dartmouth, described by the King as 'very firm as to the alteration of the Council of Massachusetts Bay'.[5] George himself was eager now to defend the rights of Parliament, where in earlier times he had preferred conciliatory policies and the avoidance of conflict. Here, as on so many occasions, the King reflected the attitudes of his subjects. Burke wrote, 'the popular current, both within doors and without, at present sets strongly against America'.[6]

The Boston Port Act was introduced on 14 March 1774. It proposed to close Boston harbour from 1 June and move the customs house to Salem until such time as Boston paid indemnity to the East India Company and compensated royal officers injured in property or person in the execution of their duty. The Bill met little opposition, even Barré giving it wholehearted support. Of the Rockinghams only Richmond, a Rockingham by birth but not, in his extreme radicalism, by conviction, denounced the Bill thoroughly, the rest believing such an affront to property and to the King's Peace should be punished, though fearful of the consequences. Franklin, an interested observer, wrote that 'the violent destruction of the tea seems to have united all parties here against our province'.[7] The Bill passed with no division.

The next two pieces of legislation did create more opposition from the Rockinghams, and Chatham also entered the fray, but with no collaborative effort, as usual. The Massachusetts Bay Regulating Act, introduced on 15 April, overthrew the charter of 1694. It replaced the elected council with a nominated one, gave the sole right to appoint and dismiss law officers to the Governor and forbade town meetings without royal consent. The system of juries' election by freeholders was abolished. The Impartial Administration of Justice Act empowered the Governor to remove certain trials to another colony or even to England.

Dowdeswell, whose fears about the consequences of coercion are well documented, accused the ministers of 'not now contending for a point of honour, you are struggling for a most ridiculous superiority';[8] and most of the Marquess's followers disapproved, as had George III on another occasion, of tampering with charters. The Bill was debated hotly; but it was Dunning for the Chathamites and Shelburnites who led the opposition to the Bill, supported by Burke and Conway but haltingly, and it was Chatham who led the charge against the Justice Bill. Even so Dunning's opposition to the Regulating Bill was defeated by 239 votes to 64, and the Justice Bill secured a majority of 127 to 24. In the Lords, perhaps because of the intervention of the ineffective Rockingham, the measures secured large majorities of 92 against 20 and 43 against 12 respectively.

Among the Intolerable Acts the colonists, and many opponents of administration, included the Quebec Act, hotly opposed in the Commons by Rockinghamites and Chathamites. It was of course part of the long-debated solution to the frontier problem and the threat posed by a large foreign and Catholic presence in North America. It was a statesmanlike measure in its grant of legislative powers, of free exercise of the Roman Catholic religion and in its recognition of Quebec's separate civil law tradition. But to the other colonists the extension of Quebec's boundaries down the Ohio to the Mississippi seemed like a punishment and a threat. It blocked expansion and outraged America's Protestant tradition. But, although the opposition divided the House eight times, the measure secured ready assent.

The Coercive Acts reached Boston on 6 August. In September George III dissolved Parliament. October was an election month, but America did not disturb even the tenor of a typical eighteenth-century election. Though the number of contested elections was unusually high at 98 in the whole country, America does not seem to have been an issue, even in these. Only among city radicals, influenced by the Bill of Rights Society and, not surprisingly, at Bristol, the constituency of Edmund Burke and a city whose prosperity owed much to colonial trade, did it feature largely. News of America's response came through during the election, and Dartmouth had foreknowledge of likely resistance as early as August. While the British political scene settled down to electioneering or summer slumber the colonists prepared themselves for a fight.

The King's assent to the Intolerable Acts, and particularly to the Quebec Act, was seen by the Essex Gazette in Massachusetts (August 1774) as ending all hope of redress. 'If the King violates his sacred Faith to, and compact with any one State of his Empire, he discharges the same from their allegiance to him, dismembers them from the Empire and reduces them to a state of Nature.' This might be 'Locke for Beginners', but it nevertheless epitomises the almost total loss of faith in the connection with Britain, and by 1775 George III had already assumed in American eyes the position from which even now they seem reluctant to pluck him, as the centre of the design for despotism which the colonists believed they saw.

The colonists made the cause of Massachusetts and Boston their own. County and provincial conventions met and passed resolutions, and for the first time the struggle against British despotism was joined by those living beyond the eastern seaboard towns. The Continental Congress of Inter-Colonial Committees of Correspondence met in Philadelphia on 5 September, and although it was not entirely radical and independence was still two years away, the old Empire was dead. Radical organisation in the committees and in the Sons of Liberty were at work with persuasion and all forms of coercion to radicalise America. Britain did the rest. The Congress adopted a Declaration of Rights and Resolves and rejected all acts affecting the 'life, liberty and property of the people of all the colonies' while continuing to accept British regulation of the external trade of the colonies. It voted addresses to the people of Britain and the other colonies, petitioned the King, and prohibited British imports from December 1774 and exports to Britain from September 1775. Although this was essentially a compromise, rejecting so far the Suffolk Resolution for an army to be formed, the essential demands made were destructive of the Empire as it had hitherto been understood. They and the effects of radical coercion of loyalists and moderates, possibly still a majority of Americans, emphasised the truth of John Adams's famous assertion that 'the revolution was complete, in the minds of the people, and the union of the Colonies, before the war commenced in the skirmishes of Concord and Lexington on 14 April 1775'. This does not mean that independence was yet demanded; but rejection of American claims would make it inevitable, and Britain simply could not accept those claims.

The government was appalled by the response to the Intolerable Acts and its patent failure to isolate Boston from a disapproving colonial majority. But to the vital question of what to do next reactions were mixed. George III was consistent in his belief that firm application of the acts would eventually bring the colonists to see reason. He sought no further punishments, but he saw the value of steady resolve. North and Dartmouth sought to avoid an appeal to force, as did Sandwich, who was only too well aware of the weakness of the navy and the potential threat from vengeful Bourbon unity. But even these conciliatory ministers were aware not only of George III's views, which could hardly be ignored on an issue of such constitutional importance, but also of the opinion in Parliament which was shocked by Boston's continued defiance and lawlessness. Within the ministry also there were those, formerly Bedfordites in the main, who looked to firm action.

On the other hand the administration was painfully conscious that it simply could not find anything like the 20 000 soldiers demanded by Gage, or the extra naval forces needed. Far from pushing the colonists into rebellion the administration allowed itself to be pushed, and its policy fell between two stools. The government decided in January 1775 to send Generals Howe, Clinton and Burgoyne with three regiments of infantry and one of cavalry plus three ships of the line to Gage, enough to excite fears of repression among colonists, insufficient to act decisively to quell rebellion. It also offered to give up the right to tax in return for American payment of colonial defence and administrative costs. Meanwhile a blockade of New England was prepared by the Trade Restraints Act of February. Such measures were insufficiently conciliatory, but gave colonists the feeling that the government lacked a strong will.

In any case, British conciliatory moves were undermined by what happened in America. Dartmouth, though anxious for peace and favouring the sending of commissioners to negotiate with representatives of Congress, a policy rejected by King and ministers in January, believed that Gage should not stay on the defensive entirely once reinforced and, as with all his colleagues, was convinced that Loyalists would rally to a strong assertion of royal authority, a view reinforced by requests for strong action by Loyalists. Gage's attempts to locate stocks of rebel arms at Concord led to the first shots of the war at Lexington and Concord on 19 April which provoked Americans everywhere to shoulder arms. In May, Ethan Allen and Benedict Arnold seized the royal forts at Ticonderoga and Crown Point; in June, Washington was put in command of a colonial army to aid Massachusetts and on 17 June the battle of Bunker's Hill occurred.

Such coherent policy as the North administration had laboured to agree on by January 1775 was therefore outstripped by events. In May the second Continental Congress met in the shadow of Lexington and Concord, hardly in the mood to accept North's offers of conciliation prepared in January. Its 'Declaration of the Causes of Taking up Arms' in July, although accompanied by the Olive Branch Petition to the King, left almost no room for manoeuvre. The denial of any desire for independence implied that such a step was now a real possibility, though Pennsylvania's assembly instructed its delegates not to vote for it. In Britain the response of MPs to Chatham's resolutions for the withdrawal of coercive measures and for statutory limitations to parliamentary sovereignty showed how unpopular such ideas were and North could never ignore the conservatism of independents. Far more pleasing to their ears were the sentiments expressed in Dr Johnson's *Taxation no Tyranny*, emphasising the indivisible nature of sovereignty.

In October 1774, when he heard of the activities of the first

Continental Congress, North had written '. . . now the case seems desperate Parliament will not/cannot concede. For aught I can see it must come to violence' and the King had been of the opinion that 'blows must decide whether they are to be subject to this country or independent'.[9] How much more likely it was by the summer of 1775 that a war to prevent independence would now follow. North's gamble on a successful assertion of limited force had failed and he was faced with the possibility of a long war, perhaps involving Spain and France, for which the country was totally unprepared.

The ill news from Lexington and Concord was confirmed in June 1775; the débâcle at Bunker Hill, the siege of Boston and the loss of the two forts were known about some seven weeks after the events. The Olive Branch Petition was, not surprisingly, rejected. Dartmouth's plea that the government should send Viscount Howe to America to negotiate, on the basis of the Petition, a revival of his earlier idea to send commissioners to negotiate with Congress, was rejected. Perhaps this was a missed opportunity but it was difficult for the ministry to negotiate with a body claiming to represent all the colonists and, as such, claiming equality with Parliament, and the Petition had been sent with little expectation of success, so its rejection was largely in the spirit of its creation.

Dartmouth's idea of sending commissioners was eventually agreed by the King in February 1776, a year after the original proposal had first been rejected. By then Congress had heard of the rejection of the Olive Branch Petition and all hope in the King had been finally abandoned. George's defence of Parliament's rights had always been total and colonial hopes that he would somehow act on their behalf illusory. The commissioners did not arrive in America until June 1776 because Dartmouth's successor as colonial secretary, Lord George Germain, insisted that the instructions given to the commissioners, the Howe brothers, should require colonial acceptance of Parliament's right to legislate before negotiations could begin. Thus, to the end, Britain's response to the colonists' actions was an uneasy, but perhaps inevitable, combination of tough talking and fond hopes of peaceful solutions.

The Declaration of Independence, the Royal Proclamation of August 1776 and the King's speech of October – which declared that a state of rebellion existed and urged Parliament to take decisive action – at least seemed to end the uncertainty. The resignations of Dartmouth and Grafton, unable to contemplate war, seemed to offer the hope of great ministerial commitment to the heavy task ahead. Opposition condemnation of the King's speech and Burke's second conciliation proposals in November met with heavy defeat, underlining wide support for military action.

Thomas Jefferson, that zealously virtuous Founding Father, wrote after the Intolerable Acts, 'though simple acts of tyranny may be ascribed to the accidental opinions of the day . . . a series of oppressions, begun at a distinguished period and pursued unalterably through every change of ministers, too plainly prove a deliberate and systematical plan of reducing us to slavery'.[10] There was no such plan. As we have seen, ministers and King constantly drew back from confrontation. The Stamp Act was repealed; the Townshend duties all but. Impositions placed on America were consistently lower than those imposed by similar taxes on the British population. The Intolerable Acts were applied only when less general measures were found to be unavailable. As Jefferson points out, ministers of every complexion shared attitudes, but they were not repressive ones, and there is no discernible difference between the actions of ministers dominated by 'Friends of America' and those with harsher attitudes. The ministers had no 'settled fixed plan for enslaving the colonies' but they did share common assumptions, almost to a man.

In the twentieth century the British tradition of parliamentary democracy is the result of three centuries of the development and maintenance of parliamentary sovereignty. In the nineteenth and twentieth centuries gradually a greater and greater proportion of the population was deemed 'fit to be brought within the pale of the constitution' (Gladstone). That constitution was an object of pride even to those who did not share in political power, and withstood the French Revolution and the Industrial Revolution. It was eminently flexible and seen as the guarantor of the liberties of English people. In the eighteenth century the happy balance of monarchy, aristocracy and 'democracy' was seen as the surety for liberty. Small wonder therefore that the defence of that stability won and upheld against Charles I, James II, foreign hostility and Jacobitism was seen as essential. But in addition that happy constitution had enabled Britain to win an Empire. So the English political élite and, as far as we can judge, the bulk of discoverable public opinion was united in defence of sovereignty over the colonies and saw the colonists as the aggressors. Had not colonists traded with the enemy? Had they not failed to help the army in the war? Had they not refused to make sufficient financial provision during the war? Did they not offer to pay external taxes and then renege on their word? Were they not guilty of coercion, social, economic and physical, of Americans loyal to the King? From the King to the country gentlemen, from the gentlemen to the freeholder there was near unanimity in hostility to American pretensions, as Franklin had pointed out. Americans looked to Britons to rise against the persecution of Wilkes in vain. To Americans this was proof of the decline of liberty in Britain:

> If bound unto that land of liberty,
> I just described, then it is not nigh
> but lies far distant from this place somewhere,
> Not in this, but some other hemisphere

wrote New Yorker Lewis Morris in 1736.[11]

But in Britain liberty itself was founded on Parliament's sovereignty and the constitution was the best in the world. In denying it the Americans threatened British liberties and British colonial supremacy. With that they raised the power of France and Spain.

There was no settled design. There was bewilderment and growing anger and frustration in Britain's rulers. Their perception of events was of course very different from the American perception but the tragedy, with hindsight, lies in two peoples driven to fight for principle, unwillingly for the most part. It is true that on one side there were Grenville and Townshend eager to establish the right to tax, and on the other Sam Adams, James Otis, Patrick Henry driven by motives, in many cases less honourable, of seeking what was tantamount to independence. But for the most part conflict was not sought, and it is symptomatic of the realisation on both sides of the enormity of the issues that Britain should still be seeking peace in summer 1776 and that America should declare its independence only after a year of bitter fighting.

The Conduct of the War 1776–82

If we are to take John Adams's view seriously Britain had lost the colonies by 1775 and the war that followed was merely a painful way of learning that lesson. It is clear that Lord North alone did not lose the colonies. The fault, if fault is the right word to use, lay not with individuals but with the British political nation. Nevertheless, North has been blamed for losing the war, and yet it was a war which could not have been won, though it need not have been so humiliatingly lost. This is not the place to write a history of the conflict, but the question of North's own responsibility for the defeat is important.

In the Seven Years' War Britain's success in America owed something to her European ally, Frederick the Great, and more to her naval supremacy. In the War of Independence Britain found herself from 1778, after Burgoyne's defeat at Saratoga, fighting France and Spain and later Holland. But this isolation owed nothing to the North administration's diplomatic errors. Pitt had failed in 1766 to secure an alliance with Prussia for the very good reason that an alliance with Britain held no obvious advantages for Prussia. Nor for that matter for Russia or Austria. Poland and Turkey exercised the minds of those powers at this time and Britain could have secured an alliance with Russia only at unacceptable cost in financial, diplomatic and naval terms. It was a general truth of the eighteenth and nineteenth centuries that when the three Eastern powers concentrated on the problem of Eastern Europe British foreign policy found itself in difficulties against a bellicose France.

It is anyway doubtful whether Britain's lack of a land ally in Europe was of crucial importance. Certainly the ministry did not think it worth paying the price for an alliance demanded by Holland, nor to keep Spain neutral by giving up Gibraltar. A European ally might well have brought the complicating issue of the need to protect Hanover into a war from which it remained mercifully absent, and George III was no less keen on preserving his family's patrimony than his grandfather and great-grandfather. Austria had long been a European ally but she was a liability from 1740 to 1748. Prussia was useful in the Seven Years' War because she, like Britain, felt that she was fighting for her life and did not let diplomatic considerations get in the way of her struggle for survival until the peril had passed, at which point it became a moot point as to whether Britain or Prussia would be the first to desert its ally.

Certainly French involvement in the continental land war in 1756 diverted resources which she could have applied to the naval conflict, but America was not won on the plains of Germany. Success there obviated the need to give back territorial gains in the colonies in order to recover Hanover, but it was naval superiority preventing France reinforcing her colonial armies which defeated her in America, with the assistance given by Americans fighting for Britain. At no time in the Seven Years' War did Britain have to take on the joint fleets of Spain and France or add to their enemies Dutch ships of the line. By the time Spain entered that war France's maritime power was defeated for the duration of the conflict. In the War of American Independence between 1778 and 1782 Britain was outweighed at sea.

The question of the extent to which the ministry was to

blame for losing the war seems less easy to understand now than it would have seemed at the end of the last century, or in the case of Sandwich until very recently. Criticism centres on four people: the King, North, Germain and Sandwich.

Sandwich's reputation as a rake and gambler has been allowed to cloud his reputation as First Lord. He was one of the most experienced First Lords in history, having served in the office before. As an administrator it is now clear that he was one of the most able holders of the post. He did not neglect the navy in peacetime. Finding only fifteen ships of the line fit for active service in 1770 he had a fleet of 100 such ships in 1779, more than were serving twenty years before.[12] But between 1778 and 1782 Britain lost control of the seas. The main problem was that the fleet had too much to do. The protection of merchant shipping against hundreds of privateers found the navy short of frigates. The need to blockade New England, deal with two enemy fleets after 1779, maintain a presence in the West Indies, the Atlantic, and Mediterranean oceans and escort ships carrying supplies to the army in America were all too much for the navy to cope with. And yet, Sandwich's fleet did defeat Spain and France at Les Saintes in 1782, and while it was true that the navy was exhausted by then, the navies of its enemies were in a worse state. Sandwich's building programme between 1778 and 1782 was enormous and it was not his fault that between 1775 and 1778 there was no building programme at all. That was the result of Treasury stringency and political decisions about the likelihood of a war for America for which the blame lies elsewhere. Certainly his management of the navy caused the King to tell North, who endeavoured to promote Sandwich from the Admiralty in 1778, 'I cannot think it wise and just to remove him'.

But Sandwich was a political liability. Admiral Rodney's question, 'can I trust that man with my honour or put my trust in him?'[13] might be discounted, coming as it did from a man ill, proud, quarrelsome and vindictive, but even Admirals such as Howe and Keppel, who at first admired him, all fell out with their political boss and he seems to have upset the navy by his appointments. Many were poor; he was accused of relying on nonentities and of not supporting his officers, charges with some truth in them. Perhaps the navy could not trust a politician in the way that they had trusted Anson. 'The fleet will now be united and want none of its best officers', wrote Horace Walpole on the fall of Sandwich.[14]

As a strategist he was essentially sound, insisting that the main threat was in home waters. As an administrator he seems to have been peerless. As a man he inspired no trust. Much the same might be said of Lord George Germain, except that his strategic sense has been most questioned. Anxious to take the offensive in America, he frequently quarrelled with the defensive strategy favoured and required by Sandwich. He might be forgiven for failing to keep proper control of the plans for 1777 which led General Howe to distract the navy for a futile and costly expedition against Philadelphia while Burgoyne struggled towards Albany, expecting Howe's help, only to meet with the humiliation of surrender at Saratoga. It was not Germain's fault that Howe adopted a third plan instead of the two which Germain had agreed to, but it was Germain's fault that he did not question the wisdom of a forward military policy at all in this area since it would never achieve much, given that the chances of holding the Hudson River–Lake Champlain route were negligible in the long run, or at least costly. Germain understood the need for a strong controlling hand on the ministry's war policy but, with his controversial military career, after the Minden court martial, he was not the man for the job. He had little real authority over the generals who though not inspired were not particularly incompetent, winning some notable victories in set-piece battles against the American armies of Washington and others. Thus although Saratoga, in persuading France to enter the war, is one of the decisive British defeats in history and Washington won victories at Princeton and Trenton, he was never able to take New York. General Howe seized Philadelphia, Cornwallis won major victories at Camden and Guilford Court House, and all invasions of Canada were routed. It is, anyway, a foolish historian who imagines that defeat and victory in wars can be explained by blanket praise or denigration of the generals of particular conflicts. In this way British generals of 1914–18 and 1776–82 have been similarly mistreated. Circumstances can ruin the efforts of the ablest commander.

What was not sufficiently realised was the logistical problem of this war.[15] The unreliability of supplies for horses and men from within America and their vulnerability to attack from American irregulars made this conflict quite different from that of the Seven Years' War. It required an army to protect those who went out to secure supplies for another army and in the end regular supplies could only be guaranteed from Britain. When the French army reached America it could live off the land and it received all the help it needed from the natives of the colonies. This forced Britain on to the defensive and the generals and Germain were quite wrong in their offensive strategy, especially if, as in the Philadelphia campaign, it distracted the navy from its blockading duties, preventing privateers getting out and arms getting in. The forward policy was partly based on a belief in the poor fighting qualities of American regulars: 'Tis not as yet, thank God, the strength of America which we fear when put in competition with this country. She has neither army, navy, money nor men', wrote the Hon. John St John, MP for Eye.[16] There persisted also an exaggerated idea of the numbers of Loyalists and their willingness to show their hand without real security. Such a belief led Howe to seize Philadelphia. But this security the army could never guarantee in what amounted to guerilla warfare. In consequence Loyalists were quickly demoralised and kept their heads down.

Sandwich and Germain were not wholly responsible for the appalling lack of unity among and between generals and admirals. The problem was partly one of conscience. Certain officers, such as Amherst, disapproved of the war and refused to serve. Admiral Keppel, a Rockinghamite MP, refused to serve against the colonists but, initially a friend of Sandwich's, he agreed to command the channel fleet in the event of a European war. In 1778 he avoided battle with a larger enemy fleet, considering that his own was deficient in power, equipment and training, and after a later inconclusive battle off Ushant he provoked a quarrel with a particular favourite of Sandwich, Admiral Palliser. Keppel's subsequent court martial became an affair of party politics which drove a deep wedge into the navy and damaged Sandwich's standing still further, though he seems to have acted honourably throughout.

But the failure of generals and admirals to work together was endemic. Rodney quarrelled with Admirals Arbuthnot, Parker and Hood. Hood was third choice to serve as Rodney's second-in-command, others, according to Sandwich, having been 'rendered unsuitable for their factious connections'.[17] Such quarrels contributed to the failure in 1781 to destroy de Grasse in the West Indies and thus to the disasters of Chesapeake and Yorktown. General Clinton and Admiral Arbuthnot communicated with each other only through a third party. But if Sandwich and Germain did not create, and could hardly have always prevented, such bitter divisions, their own ill relations and inability to inspire trust in colleagues and subordinates must have contributed to them.

Perhaps if Britain had acted more decisively at the beginning of the war things might have been better. Germain, Dartmouth's successor, had urged this. But there were difficulties inherent in an un-military country like Britain of raising armies in a hurry, and recruitment in Britain was not helped by the King's gentlemanly insistence that private regiments must not be raised before older regiments had achieved their full strength. But the blame must also fall on North. The lack of naval building between 1775 and 1778 was a result of North's unwillingness to raise money and his gamble that war would be avoided, or if it happened, would be short, either because of early victory or, more likely, negotiation. Thus the peace commission, sent in 1778 under the Earl of Carlisle, was an attempt to conduct diplomacy in the eighteenth century way of talking once each side had delivered a few blows at the other. The Howe brothers can be

1776 in the attack on Long Island to be deliberately
ng inflicting a devastating defeat on Washington,
could have been achieved, in the hope that some kind
of negotiated settlement could still be arrived at.

After Saratoga, North's gamble had been lost. The effect
on him is only too plain to see. Nevertheless it is important
that he should not be loaded with too much responsibility.
Eighteenth century government was a government of departments. George II had once reminded Newcastle that
there was no such office as that of Prime Minister. Germain
might compare North with Pitt to the latter's advantage, but
in the first place Pitt did not have to bear the burdens of the
Treasury, and in the second it is now quite clear from the
work of such historians as Dr Middleton[18] that Pitt's own
supposed role as some sort of supremo, on the lines of
Winston Churchill in World War II, will not bear the light of
evidence. Not only did Pitt not interfere in departments,
such as the Admiralty, but he did not make innovations in
command or control of the war effort at all. Since so much of
what Pitt is supposed to have done is myth it is a little hard to
criticise North for failing to copy it. In the Seven Years' War,
the First Lord of the Treasury restricted himself to raising
money. North did more, but there was no precedent for a
war supremo, unless we count the first Marlborough, in
rather different circumstances.

As First Lord, North was considerably stretched. He
reminded the King in 1778 that 'to perform the duties of the
Treasury, to attend the House of Commons at the rate of
three long days a week, to see the numbers of persons who
have daily business with the First Lord of the Treasury and
to give all thought to the principal measures of government
in this very alarming crisis is enough to employ the greatest
man of business, and the most consummate statesman that
ever existed, and is infinitely more than Lord North can
undertake'.[19] There is much truth in North's self-
justification. Only Pitt the Younger combined the work of
First Lord and war minister with any success in the eighteenth century and his record as war minister is open to

question, while his alcoholism and early death are perhaps testimony to the heavy weight of responsibility.

In his prime duties, raising money and coping with increased Treasury responsibility for supplying the troops in America, North was remarkably successful. Contemporaries levelled criticism at the corruption involved, particularly in government relations with contractors, but the remedy of open bidding for contracts would have entailed a dangerous change of gear in mid-war with possibly damaging consequences, and the amount of corruption was greatly exaggerated. The total cost of the war was £124 million. Lotteries and annuities helped to keep the cost of raising the money down in a period of rising interest rates. North was no reformer, for he had no opportunity during the war, but it was his own response to opposition demands for an enquiry into the civil list in 1780 which created the Parliamentary Commission on Public Accounts from which so many of the financial and administrative reforms of the 1780s flowed.

Nonetheless in North's letter to the King there is an element of special pleading. There seem to be expectations of North as head of the ministry which he is not fulfilling. And if North was not to take hold of affairs who could? He would not and did not take responsibility. He seems to have played little part in cabinet discussion of military matters. As a matter of departmental responsibility this can be excused, but when the ministry showed increasing signs of disintegrating he did nothing to hold it together. His responses were two: after Saratoga for two years he spoke constantly of resignation; alternatively he spoke of ministerial reshuffles. Neither did he successfully accomplish, and the attempts at both made his ministry less and less cohesive, more and more obviously an appalling sea of conflicting tides and currents.

'Damn him ... nothing can goad him forward. He is the very clog that loads everything', wrote Lord Chancellor Thurlow of North.[20] In 1778 (March) North urged the King to send for Chatham and in 1779 he seems to have briefly and ineffectively attempted an approach to some of the Rockinghams through Fox, Grafton and Camden. He urged his own retirement on the King in May 1778 and on four separate occasions in 1779. But never did he insist on anything, so nothing changed – except for the worse.

Divisions and lack of confidence in North's leadership bedevilled ministerial relations. For six months after the Earl of Suffolk's death in March 1779 North was unable to find a new Secretary of State. The Bedfordites, Gower and Weymouth, resigned in the autumn of 1779, tired of North's dilatoriness and indecisiveness. Meanwhile, the Reverend Christopher Wyvill's movement for economic and parliamentary reform which began in 1779 suggested an undercurrent of discontent with the ministry which was reflected in Parliament in the success of the Shelburnite MP John Dunning's famous motion of April 1780 'that the influence of the Crown has increased, is increasing and ought to be diminished.' Sympathy with Keppel on his acquittal was reflected not only in public demonstrations but in the large though unsuccessful vote for Sandwich's dismissal in 1779. North's own deep respect for the House of Commons and his attention to its moods, especially where independent country gentlemen were concerned, added to his paralysis and despair.

It is only fair to point out that to add to all his other preoccupations North was beset by Ireland. There, Irish Whig Patriots under Henry Grattan in the Dublin Parliament, sympathising with the Americans, allies of the Rockinghams, and seeing their own relationship with Westminster writ large in the colonial struggle, were only too prepared to make trouble for North. A trade depression and a sympathetic viceroy led the government to try to make trade concessions to the Irish. Some were accepted in Parliament but a merchant lobby was so effective and North's position so precarious, that he allowed the chief measure, the Irish Import Bill, to be killed off in the Lords. The Irish Volunteer Movement, soon numbering several thousand armed Irish patriots, made North's position very awkward. Caught between stubborn English manufacturers, avowed Irish patriots and pressure for action from the Rockinghams, North's only solution was to allow Irish non-importation agreements and the threat of armed resistance in Ireland to wring concessions from industrialists. It was not a heroic or positive policy but by 1780 it had worked. Briefly in 1780 North seemed to have reached calmer waters.

The King insisted throughout that North should remain in office and he did not cease to give wholehearted support to his minister. North had more patronage at his disposal than any of his predecessors and as the First Lord's confidence ebbed it was the King who did most to bolster his flagging spirits. In 1779, with the Keppel affair at its height, the cabinet incapable of acting with purpose or unity, Spain now an enemy, and the Irish showing signs of rebelliousness, the King wrote a long letter to North underlining the necessity of carrying on the war. 'Should America succeed in that [independence] the West Indies must follow them ... Ireland would soon follow the same plan and be a separate state. Then this island would be a poor island indeed ...'[21] Of an extraordinary meeting of the cabinet summoned to meet him, George demanded 'firmness and support'.

The King insisted therefore that the war be seen through to a successful conclusion and made it clear that he could neither contemplate nor discover any alternative first minister. But because his chosen minister lacked confidence the King was obliged to become more and more involved in the work of the ministry and to supply the want of leadership. 'If others will not be active, I must drive', wrote the King to Sandwich.[22]

It was the King who insisted therefore in May 1778 that North continue in a position which the latter had declared himself incapable of maintaining. It was the King who put an end to North's attempt to promote Sandwich out of harm's way in 1778 and therefore prevented any serious deal being made with the opposition. The King was prepared to permit members of opposition groups to enter the ministry and indeed sanctioned negotiations, but he would never permit the terms which alone would have made their accession possible.

It is easy to argue that the King was wrong to insist on North remaining in a position which he seems so ill-equipped to fill. But this view ignores too many facts. The support for the war and its purpose which the King demonstrates was shared in full by most of the political nation until Yorktown. Only then did King and Parliament really lose touch with each other. Given this, it is not easy to suggest any alternative to North. No one else in the Commons had his combination of managerial and debating skill and his financial acumen. Charles James Fox, leading ally of Rockingham after his dismissal from the Treasury Board in 1774, had oratorical skill and a wayward brilliance, but he was lazy and personally objectionable to the King, while his opinion that America should be granted independence without conditions was unacceptable to the majority opinion in Parliament. It is also important to remember that North's confidence fluctuated from day to day and week to week, and his stated desire to resign was not followed up by any action until 1782. As the King pointed out in 1778, 'you want to retire and yet will not take the first step towards enabling me to arrange matters that I may acquiesce in your request.'[23] It is hardly surprising therefore that the King's response to North's inadequacies was to try to give North strong support and to fill the deficiencies as much as possible himself.

It cannot be said that by 1780 North's ministry was strong. Sandwich and Germain were not political assets and the replacements for Weymouth, Suffolk and Gower were not of equal weight. Many of North's immediate difficulties were past in 1780, though not because of any decisive action on his part. The boycott of British trade by Ireland had finally allowed him to solve the most immediate Irish problem; the Gordon Riots in June 1780 set back the Wyvill Movement and warned conservative men off extra-parliamentary activities; the battle of Camden, 16 August 1780, in which Cornwallis annihilated the army of General Gates, seemed to suggest that victory was still possible in America. North's calling of an election in 1780 caught the opposition wrong-footed and, of course, the election was a victory for the administration. But although £50 000 was spent North's majority was not greatly improved, and in open constituencies candidates supporting the administration did poorly. He survived the session of 1781 quite well with the opposition showing little desire to challenge on America. But Yorktown finally convinced a majority that victory was impossible and sealed North's fate. Warned by independents that they could no longer support him he resigned in March 1782 and left a more than reluctant monarch to accept the inevitable, a Rockingham/Shelburne ministry. North had fallen, but not as a result of the triumphant efforts of opposition. They merely succeeded, *faut de mieux*, to an empty seat.

North's administration was a poor war ministry but it suffers too much from comparison with the Pitt–Newcastle ministry. In fact, that ministry's victory could never be repeated for it took place in peculiar circumstances, but it contributed most to the myth that defeat must be the result of incompetence, corruption or treachery. As a naval power Britain was, and proved herself again in 1782, supreme, but a naval power is not a world power, for a navy cannot do to a land power what armies are able to do, and that is to be decisive. It is often forgotten that Britain could operate with armies in America in the Seven Years' War with two-thirds of her troops being provided by the very people who, with French military help in addition, defeated her in 1781. Britain by 1782 had defeated the navies of her old enemies in Europe. No doubt she could have resumed the war against the colonies, making blockade effective; she would find it well nigh impossible to defeat them on land. But the question is academic. The political will to attempt it had gone. The new ministry was committed to independence.

4
THE FAILURE OF OPPOSITION 1770–82

The chief reasons for the failure of the opposition to the American policy of North's administration lay in the near unanimity of political support for parliamentary sovereignty, which has been detailed sufficiently in the preceding chapters, the divisions within the parliamentary opposition, the weakness of extra-parliamentary movements and the pressures of patriotism reinforced by the entry of the Bourbon powers into the arena.

To follow the unhappy thoughts and fears of the Earl of Dartmouth between 1770 and 1775 is to begin to understand the dilemma of the Rockinghams with whom politically he was most closely allied. Well-disposed towards the Americans, and genuinely anxious to avoid conflict, he nonetheless accepted the coercive legislation of 1774, for the government was upholding the letter, if not the spirit of the Declaratory Act. The Rockinghamites shared royal and Northite belief in the sovereignty of Parliament which made it difficult for them to oppose government policy. The argument that Parliament should not assert its rights if they met with too much opposition from America – or as Burke put it 'you are not bound to exercise every right you possess. Your prudence should regulate the exercise of your power'[1] – found little favour in the House of Commons. Arguments that the colonies were not in a state of rebellion in 1775 were palpably false and British concessions did not, by 1775, meet the colonists' advancing demands.

Rockinghamite numbers were too few anyway to make inroads on a ministry strongly backed by the Crown and in general well-favoured by the independent country gentlemen. The Rockinghamite connection, though given greater unity by its sad numerical decline since 1765, was hardly 'lean and hungry' and not yet a real party. The members were too aristocratic to need office. It was a confederation of noble families more than a party and kept together by a remarkable degree of loyalty to Rockingham. But when he was absent in Yorkshire, improving his estates and proudly showing his guests his steaming piles of horse manure, the Rockinghamites tended to 'fall into confusion and . . . nothing but yourself has the means of rightly managing the different characters and reconciling the different interests that make up the corps of opposition'.[2]

The Rockinghamites might have been more effective if they had been able to work closely with Chatham, even though his following, largely dependent on Shelburne for most members, numbered only about a dozen. But too much history and too much principle kept them apart. Since Burke's *Thoughts on the Present Discontents* the Rockinghams had emphasised the role of party in politics. Party alone could form the basis of an effective administration, capable of avoiding the errors of Pitt's own disastrous 'tesselated pavement' ministry and withstanding the 'secret influence' wielded by the King. But 'party' had made the Rockinghams more and more exclusive and less and less to the liking of Pitt, who had never approved of party, having, in his view, suffered from it in his alliance with Newcastle, and had made it his principle not to serve with a party-based ministry ever again. In 1766 he had attempted to pulverise party; 'party' and patriotism were no more compatible than party and his own 'caesarist' style of leadership. But Chatham and the Rockinghams were divided too on policy and principle. Pitt had denounced the Declaratory Act and had, amidst the circumlocution, made a distinction, it was thought, between internal and external taxation of the colonies. He had denied Parliament an important part of its sovereignty. Chatham had always believed that there were certain fundamental rights which Parliament could not touch. It was not only over America that this led to disputes between Chatham and the Rockinghamites. On the question of whether in cases of libel the jury should decide not just the fact of publication but also the question of whether what had been written was a libel or not, the two groups were united. But while Rockingham sought to change the law in 1770–71, Chatham objected that the right of trial by jury was fundamental law which needed merely to be re-stated in legislation. The difference was slight, but it was a difference reflecting real differences of principle on the constitution. It created friction and led to the loss of a very valuable measure.

Rockingham feared all outbursts of popular politics not properly controlled by politicians such as himself, as he had amply demonstrated with the Middlesex Election Petitioning Movement of 1769–70. Any talk of parliamentary reform was to be severely deprecated. Yet in 1770 Chatham adopted a mild form of parliamentary reform, and his ally, Shelburne, through his City contacts, was a major patron of radicals like James Townsend, John Sawbridge, the Reverend Mr Horne and others. Such connections, and the collapse of all Rockinghamite influence in the City after 1770, when their City man Trecothick failed to support Wilkes and fell from favour despite his vigorous denunciation of government policy in America, drove an even deeper wedge between the two chief opposition forces in Parliament.

On top of all this it has to be said that Chatham was tiresome and unpredictable, arrogant and condescending. His ill health made his appearances in the Lords rare, uncertain and capricious. He expected others to do what he wanted and had never ceased to wish to be dictator in any coalition or ministry. He told no one of his plans, not even his faithful Sancho Panza, Shelburne, and certainly not Rockingham.

On 31 January 1775 Chatham, without informing the Rockinghamites, introduced a plan of conciliation. He asserted that an agreement could be reached on the basis of a colonial recognition of Parliament's sovereignty limited by an agreement that taxes should not be raised other than with the assent of a provincial assembly, and that as an earnest of this the Continental Congress should be recognised as representing the colonies. Congress should grant the King a revenue, and in return Parliament would withdraw all coercive legislation. It was for Chatham a remarkably clear statement, but it caught the Rockinghams totally unprepared. They felt obliged to support the scheme, though unwillingly, more to deny the administration too great a victory than because they accepted all its points. Chatham's scheme undermined the authority of Burke's first conciliation proposals, delivered on 22 March on behalf of his party.

Speaking for two and a half hours in what was recognised then as one of the great parliamentary speeches of all time he urged a pragmatic approach, unlimited by past pronouncements and legislation. Britain should give up taxation without reference to right and repeal all coercive legislation if the imperial connection was to be maintained. He reminded his hearers of the passionate American love of liberty, of the distinct personality of colonial society and of the impossibility of altering this character, especially with 3000 miles of ocean between the two competing parties. But two hours of great oratory still left him carrying only 70 votes against 270.

The obvious failure of Chatham and Rockingham to work together told against Burke, but in truth neither plan stood any chance of acceptance. Parliament would never recognise Congress as equal in the raising of taxes even if the colonists would agree to impose them. Burke's proposals to permit America to opt out of the principles of the Declaratory Act went quite beyond any eighteenth century concept of the meaning and purpose of empires, and no one in Britain really believed that the Americans would raise a revenue voluntarily. But the colonies wished to be free to raise money or not to raise it, not simply to be free to decide how. Thus their ideas of equality went far beyond what Chatham or Burke argued they were claiming. At least Chatham sought the repeal of the Declaratory Act. Even in his more far-reaching November proposals Burke retained that measure, seeking to maintain the right but not to use it. Pragmatism could go no further and its retention implied a colonial faith in Parliament's goodwill which had long before evaporated. MPs could not really comprehend what Burke was saying. If the Declaratory Act correctly asserted a right then North should be supported in defending it. Burke seemed to be arguing that one side in the dispute would make all the concessions. As Josiah Tucker, Dean of Gloucester and a pungent commentator on the American issue wrote, 'on these simple principles of simple peace-making I will engage to terminate any difference in the world'.[3]

It is hard to see that either Chatham's or Burke's proposals could be described as statesmanlike since, presumably, statesmanlike proposals ought to stand some chance of implementation. The opposition's divisions did not help, but the ideas of Burke and Chatham, like the plans of the government, were already out of time when they were promulgated. The colonists had already gone far beyond them, while the MPs lagged far behind them.

The lack of co-operation between Rockingham and Chatham owed most to Chatham's hostility to party and commitment to his own independence. In 1769 and 1770 the two leaders had at least worked together on the petitioning movement which had been organised to protest against the House of Commons' selection of Henry Lawes Luttrell as MP for Middlesex in place of the popularly elected, but legally disqualified, John Wilkes. Even here however the Chathamite association with wider social causes had created friction and by 1770 co-operation, like the petitioning movement itself, was petering out. Rockingham disapproved of the growing radicalism of the City of London, Chatham's right hand man Beckford died in 1770, and Wilkes, whom Chatham detested, was given a free hand in London. But the break up of the Bill of Rights Society in 1771, caused by the personality of Wilkes, and the emergence of calmer economic and political waters in the 1770s temporarily suspended the radical challenge such as it had been. Parliament remained immune to outside pressures. Wilkes himself, admitted to Parliament in 1774, sank slowly into insignificance. Thus neither the radical impetus provided by the City nor the tenuous link with it forged by Chatham and Rockingham survived into the period of the coercive legislation, to offer any assistance to opponents of the government's policy.

The colonists were disappointed by this and even more by the failure of British merchants to respond to the threat of non-importation. The clue to why this should be the case can be found in a letter of Colonel John Maunsell in July 1775. He wrote to his colonial correspondents, 'England was never in a more flourishing state – new doors opened to commerce, manufactures fully employed, stocks as high as before the dispute.'[4] Merchants had begun to find lucrative markets in Europe. Exports to Russia had risen by 300 per cent since the beginning of George III's reign, to France by 30 per cent,[5] while markets in America could hardly be expected to be stable again until Parliament's sovereignty was re-established. Few merchants could accept the colonists' apparent rejection of the imperial Parliament's right to regulate trade and there is no evidence that in general merchants had any sympathy with colonial constitutional arguments. Besides colonial importers, anxious to beat the deadline of non-importation, had placed good orders with British industry so there was no depression like that of 1765. Small wonder then that the Rockinghams should have difficulty in raising petitions against the coercive acts. A dozen petitions were presented but they were lame and extracted with difficulty, even in Yorkshire. 'Hence it is', wrote William Lee, agent for Virginia, 'that our petitions are almost all . . . little else than milk and water.'[6] 'We look to the merchants in vain', said Burke, 'they are gone from us and from themselves. They consider America is lost, and they look to the administration for an indemnity.'[7]

Opposition to Lord North before 1776 by Rockinghamites,

Chathamites and those outside Westminster had been divided and feeble. Because North fell in 1782 and was succeeded by an administration led by Rockingham and Shelburne it is tempting to assume that the opposition was more successful in the second half of North's premiership. In one obvious sense it was, but little that the opposition did, other than being there, brought it success. When North resigned and the war's end became inevitable there was no one else for the King to employ. The opposition's short ministerial life is proof of the weakness of its position.

The war with America made the stance of the opposition extremely difficult at first, though it promised future rewards. Patriotism and right seemed involved in the government's stand. Opposition appeared almost treasonable and it was no comfortable situation to seem likely to benefit only from Britain's defeat. Moreover, the difficulty of explaining why a party which refused to give up the Declaratory Act, even in November 1775, should find itself opposing a war fought for its principles left the Rockinghams in a quandary, and opposition to the strategy of a land war against the colonists, favoured by some in the opposition, suffered from a lack of any clear alternatives and optimism about the war. Rockingham's view that the coercion of America was another stage in the expansion of secret royal influence was not a fruitful line of argument under a popular minister fighting Parliament's cause.

Although there was an attempt in 1775 to work with Chatham, an alliance pressed by Shelburne, Camden and Grafton, it achieved nothing of importance and by the middle of 1776 the party considered seceding from Parliament altogether. The Declaration of Independence in the long run was to help the Rockinghams adopt the policy of granting independence without conditions, as the most practical action, but it was to create its own difficulties with the followers of Chatham. In the short term, support for American liberties in defence of English liberties against a tyrannical monarch had the virtue of consistency but not of popularity and it did not solve the problem of what Rockinghamite attitudes to independence were to be. Secession from Parliament, vigorously opposed by Rockingham's new ally Charles James Fox, a genuine libertarian, bitter opponent of the King, and chief author of the conspiracy theory of royal intentions towards liberty, was put off in 1776. In 1777 it was attempted, but even this limited united action proved impossible to bring off, and as the secessionists did not include Chatham's followers it merely underlined party ineptitude and opposition divisions, while giving North an easy time in Parliament.

The news of Saratoga began the release of the Rockinghams from their dilemma. It now seemed sensible to argue, as Burke and others had already tentatively been doing, that the war could not be won, that the Declaratory Act should be abandoned not as wrong but as no longer relevant and American independence unconditionally recognised, a view firmly espoused by Fox in 1778. This policy made particular sense to the Rockinghams after France's entry into the war in 1778, but unofficially even earlier, and they would argue that the country should concentrate its efforts on its old enemies and not dissipate its resources in a war it could not win, a point of view reflected in Keppel's willingness to fight in European waters but not in American. Unfortunately for the opposition, war against France and Spain raised the patriotic temperature higher, made colonial assertions that this was a war for liberty seem hollow, and consequently painted the Rockinghams in even more unflatteringly unpatriotic colours. Yet more importantly, as the Rockinghams moved cautiously towards the recognition of American independence they became increasingly estranged from Chatham and Shelburne, as Fox regretfully appreciated. The Chathamites absolutely opposed unconditional independence and this division of opinion was to dog the relationship between the two groups beyond Chatham's death in 1778, right up to the peace-making of 1783. Chatham had not built his career on the importance of Empire and trade now to give it all away. Independence without special trade concessions by America was unthinkable and he refused to discuss independence at all. Anxious to maintain good relations the Rockinghams did not press the point in 1777 but concentrated instead on advocating peace and conciliation, neither of which was achievable or new.

Relations between the two opposition groups were not helped by North's offer to Chatham to enter the ministry in 1778. Rockingham finally demanded recognition of American independence on receiving the expected news of France's alliance with America. Chatham was furious, and his anger might have contributed to his death, which left his party in the hands of Shelburne, a man of more amenable temperament but no less committed to Chatham's views on Empire, a man moreover with a strong association with City radicalism and ideas of reform, which the Rockinghams did not admire, and personally odious to the increasingly important Fox.

Within the Rockinghams themselves there was, by 1779, considerable disagreement over tactics. The eager young Fox was tired, as an outsider, latecomer and ambitious man, of party principle. It was idle, he said, 'to preserve the party's principles and virtue in a powerless opposition'.[8] He sought permission to respond to feelers put out by North for the accession to the ministry of some Rockinghamites so that others might later follow. It was foolish to suppose, he argued, that the Rockinghamites would ever form a ministry by themselves. The mainstream of Rockinghamite support refused the arguments and the very tentative offers, feeling that North would not have made any offers at all if it had not been for the significant advances made by opposition.

Such progress seemed to be enhanced during 1779 by the acquittal of Keppel, the motion of censure on Sandwich and by the threatened French invasion of June 1779, which, although it raised patriotism to fever pitch, seemed also to prove the party's contention that the war against America was now positively dangerous for national security and that the ministers were incompetent or corrupt. The greatest hope for opposition seemed however to lie in the movement founded by the Reverend Christopher Wyvill in Yorkshire, which began in 1779 and which, in its mobilisation of the disquiet and prejudices of country gentlemen, made economical reform a national demand, in tune with long-standing Rockinghamite principles and policy.

Rockinghamite belief in the King's misuse of his prerogative to advance his secret influence was the very stuff of party principle. It had the advantage, not only of explaining the failure of the party in the past and the success of North, but it also suggested reforms of a kind which made parliamentary reform – increased representation and redistribution of seats – unnecessary. We do not have to accept the party's arguments to believe that their own faith in them was genuine. From their own standpoint everything since the 'Massacre of the Pelhamite Innocents' pointed to a royal plan to undermine real Whiggism and extend royal power. In this mood the Rockinghams had in 1778 supported Philip Jennings' (Clerke's) motion for the disenfranchisement of government contractors, and they saw in the campaign led by Wyvill for public economy a movement which could focus discontent and give impetus to 'economical reform' or the removal of the means by which the King employed 'secret influence' to undermine ministries of which he disapproved, as in the Strange Affair, and keep in power those like North's which did not seem to have any reason for surviving other than royal favour. Wyvill sought public economy through the abolition of placemen, but he saw this as the first stage on the road to parliamentary reform, though not of a radical kind but firmly in the eighteenth century 'country' tradition. It was important for the Rockinghams to back the movement but to limit its objectives to the abolition of some placemen only, avoiding the dangerous implications of parliamentary reform. For Wyvill, though not trusting the Rockinghams, it was important to have the support of a party with important local political clout, though he preferred Shelburne's views, since Shelburne was a genuine patron of parliamentary reform, friend to scientists and political and religious radicals, and the one Westminster politician to have any real authority in the City. In this way the Wyvill movement, though useful to Rockingham's party, once again underlined its differences from its parliamentary ally.

The development of the Association Movement began with the Yorkshire County Meeting of 1779 (December), and from the start Rockingham sought to dominate it. The petitioning of sixteen counties and several boroughs for economy and against the influence of the Crown was followed by a much less successful movement of petitions for parliamentary reform, which the Rockinghamites did not support.

The Association Movement, as its name suggests, was not simply a petitioning movement like that of 1769. Reaching back to the Civil War and to America for inspiration it sought to set up a permanent organisation of committees in every county corresponding with each other and in 1780 created the National Association of committee representatives itself. Unfortunately for good relations between the movement and the Rockinghams, John Jebb, a Unitarian Westminster radical, attempted to expand the idea of the Association Movement into an alternative electoral system and Parliament, threatening the House of Commons as rival assemblies in the colonies had threatened, and eventually replaced, the colonial legislatures. Such ideas, popular in Westminster, antagonised the Rockinghams though not apparently Fox or Richmond, and made it difficult for Wyvill to keep both his parliamentary allies and the metropolitan and Westminster radicals within the movement. Wyvill wished to go far beyond what the Rockinghams would allow but was just as critical of threats to Parliament as most men in England, and he was all too aware of how very much such ideas offended the country gentlemen and freeholders.

Such conservatism was reinforced by the Gordon Riots of June 1780 which held London in thrall to a rampaging mob for a week and seemed to underline to most men in politics the dangers of playing with radical fire, despite the fact that these riots against Sir George Savile's Catholic Relief Act had nothing to do with radical reform. Nevertheless, before June the impetus of the movement and the unpopularity of the administration did achieve something. The Rockinghams and the Wyvillites found it impossible to work closely together, but Sir George Savile's presentation of the Yorkshire petition was followed shortly by Burke's plans for the abolition of offices serving no useful public purpose. In addition, the Bill disqualifying contractors from sitting in the House was reintroduced and Barré's scheme for an enquiry into the civil list, though neatly turned and expanded by North, maintained momentum until Dunning carried his famous motion that 'the influence of the Crown has increased, is increasing and ought to be diminished' in April. This motion had the twin virtue of being vague and acceptable to all in the reform movement.

But the limits of such an opposition were only too clearly shown by the defeat of all the rest of Dunning's motions, which the country gentlemen believed encroached on the royal prerogative, and by the easy defeat of Sawbridge's annual motion for shorter parliaments which the Rockinghamites refused to countenance. The subsequent fate of the Association Movement's campaign for parliamentary reform in the counties – only four counties accepted it – underlined that that issue remained largely metropolitan and what was metropolitan rarely endeared itself to the country gentlemen whose support it would need. The Gordon Riots completed the woes of opposition while providing new material for quarrels between Shelburne and Rockingham, when Rockingham accused Shelburne of fomenting trouble by supporting the Protestant Association, especially as it was Rockingham's ally, Savile, who had been the author of Catholic Relief. In the election of 1780 Rockingham found two Association members standing against his own sitting MPs in the city of York, underlining the weakness of the relationship. The Wyvillite movement continued for several years and spawned much of value to the growth of radicalism, but though it gave some impetus to the Rockingham programme of economical reform it did not create it, nor produce any positive results. The simple facts remained that while there might be a general feeling that only corruption could explain high taxes and failure in war, and that the administration was a poor one, there remained hope, especially after Camden, of future military success and there was little support for specific reforms, even of economical reform, and for parliamentary reform within the parliamentary system itself support was negligible. The parliamentary opposition remained divided; 'outside' opposition was as dependent on support from 'inside' as ever for success. While George III supported North and while North continued to show a willingness to serve there was no way for the opposition to replace him. When North fell he did so because the independent gentlemen would no longer support him or the war, and North was far too much of a House of Commons man to believe that he could, at the same time, serve a King who wanted to continue a war and a House of Commons that did not. Nothing suggests that when North fell there was any great enthusiasm for the men the King was forced to turn to to replace him, or for extensive programmes of economic, let alone parliamentary, reform.

5

ROCKINGHAM, SHELBURNE AND PEACE-MAKING

A Rockingham–Shelburne ministry was inevitable in 1782 because North's resignation left the King with no alternative; neither Rockingham nor Shelburne was strong enough alone and the temper of the House was to give up the unequal struggle in America, an attitude which the naval victory at Les Saintes did nothing to alter. Because the Rockingham–Shelburne ministry was in office a peace with America and her allies was inevitable, though in April 1782 Britain mastered her European enemies at sea. But the survival of this new ministry was not inevitable. It was one thing to offer independence, quite another to get both sides of the coalition to agree to the terms under which it should be offered. Even more it was difficult to present peace treaties to Parliament which it would be happy to accept, particularly after victory at sea and in the face of a powerful party still supporting Lord North.

But in the end this ministry would depend on the Closet, the command of the Treasury and of the Commons, as did all administrations. Here success was not assured. Those independents who had withdrawn support from North had transferred it to the new ministry only in the sense that they would, except in very unusual circumstances, support any administration apparently supported by the King. Only in the matter of ending a war had they backed a policy and although there might be a desire for a modicum of reform and a wish to see the power of the Crown diminished this was a conservative hope for the re-establishment of equilibrium. They did not share the Rockinghamites' hostility to the King or their obsession with 'secret influence' or party; they did wish to preserve the balance of the constitution and to do so as much against 'aristocratic faction' as against royal favourites. Few in Parliament shared Shelburnite enthusiasm for parliamentary reform.[1] There was little respect for the Rockinghamites as a party and not a few independents shared Wyvill's own suspicions of Rockinghamite ambition and pretension.

Control of the Treasury should mean control of patronage but this in turn depended on the holder of the office and on the King's attitude to him. Rockingham returned to office too late. Already ill when he became First Lord in March, he was to die on 1 July 1782 leaving Shelburne to succeed him. At no point was Rockingham given the full disposal of places. George III insisted that patronage be evenly divided. Thus from the start Rockingham lacked favour in the Closet.

During the negotiations for the ministry the King never dealt directly with Rockingham. Using Thurlow as intermediary the King, from the first, struggled to avoid being constrained by the bounds of party. On the collapse of the first negotiations the King then used Shelburne as his intermediary, thus helping to maintain some freedom of action for the future by setting up Shelburne as his preferred man in the ministry, and a man who shared royal hostility to the unpopular claims of party. From the start the Rockinghamite section of the administration therefore saw its leader denied favour in the Closet and that favour diverted to Shelburne who was assured by the King, anxious not to 'yield to the importunities of Lord Rockingham',[2] that he would have an equal share of patronage with the Marquis. After all it must be remembered that this was a coalition. But of course such duality made the ministry extremely unstable and the presence in the ministry of Thurlow, acting as the

King's eyes and ears, did not help. Fox, whose dislike of Shelburne was personal as well as political, noted that the ministry 'was to consist of two parts – one belonging to the King, the other to the public'.[3] Rockingham was soon complaining of 'want of confidence' as the workings of dual control of patronage provided a multitude of opportunities for disputes. Aware themselves of the fragility of their position the ministry sought to achieve as much as possible to reduce the power of the Crown before the sinister forces of 'secret influence' destroyed it.

Clerke's Bill to remove government contractors from the Commons was finally passed and John Crewe's Bill to disenfranchise revenue officers became law. Neither achieved anything. Government contractors numbered less than twenty and did not invariably vote with government or in any uniform way at all, while the Act left untouched the MPs with connections with the great City trading companies. Crewe's Act was badly drafted and easily circumvented.[4] Neither dented royal influence and Shelburne's own public attitude was lukewarm, while Lord Chancellor Thurlow opposed both measures. Burke's Establishment Act was the core of economic reform but it was a great deal less far-reaching than the proposals of 1780 and served again to demonstrate ministerial differences. The abolition of the Board of Trade and Secretaryship of State for the Colonies was petty in motivation and made little administrative sense; 134 Household offices, 22 tenable with a seat in the Commons, were abolished but many more, so far unused, were ready to be filled. The division of the civil list budget into eight classes each with an official responsible for budgeting was based upon the entirely false notion that royal corruption had its centre there. The measure proved that Burke had no eye for administrative reform and the measure soon proved a nightmare. A. S. Foord in *The Waning of the Influence of the Crown* has demonstrated that Crown power and patronage remained undisturbed. It was seen at the time as innovatory but did little to increase the weight of the Commons in the balance against the Crown, especially as the Crown's control of honours and peerages remained sacrosanct.

Already economic reform had demonstrated divisions in the cabinet. Parliamentary reform created new tensions. The Duke of Richmond's own radicalism ran to five out of the six points of the famous radical charter of 1838, only the 'ungentlemanly' ballot being denied, and Shelburne's own position was well known, though his enthusiasm for reform had been less evident since becoming royal favourite. Fox, with his leading position in the Westminster Association – noted for its radical leanings – was also when it suited him not averse to the idea. Rockingham acceded to Richmond's demand for a motion for a parliamentary enquiry to be set up but in the vote of May 1782, initiated by Pitt the Younger at the behest of Richmond and Wyvill for a committee to study the state of representation, the Rockinghamites split down the middle, infuriating Richmond and causing Fox to lose interest in reform though not before making a thinly veiled attack on Shelburne.

The House of Commons showed itself already apathetic towards economic reform and hostile to parliamentary reform. The granting of legislative independence to Ireland in the aftermath of Yorktown and under Volunteer pressure won the ministry no new support, upset the King and showed Shelburne ominously silent; but America was to provide the issue which was to destroy a ministry already lacking popularity, royal favour or unity, even within the Rockingham party.

Fox was Secretary of State for Foreign Affairs, Shelburne Secretary of State for Home and Colonial business. In peace negotiations with America, France and Spain it would have been difficult anyway for the two men to work together. But these were not just any two politicians; they were two of the most controversial of their respective generations; they disliked each other intensely, they were divided by royal favour and, even worse, by different views of peace-making. While Fox wished to offer immediate independence to America, without conditions, on principle and in order to undo the damage of the Franco–American Alliance, Shelburne, in the

Chatham tradition, wished to make that independence conditional on peace and on commercial concessions. Benjamin
Franklin was able to play off the two ministers against each
other through their representatives, Richard Oswald in the
case of Shelburne, and Thomas Grenville in the case of Fox.
The cabinet – which might have been expected to settle the
issue – gave Shelburne on 23 April leave to offer conditional
terms, and on 23 May, after hearing of Les Saintes, gave Fox
leave to tell the French that unconditional independence was
on offer. Of course these were not seen to be contradictory
offers, merely bargaining positions, but as Fox ignored the
first cabinet decision and Shelburne the second they did
nothing to help peace-making or relations between the two
secretaries.

Fox's conviction of Shelburne's duplicity in this matter was
reinforced by royal support for Shelburne's bargaining position, an attitude totally in keeping with long-held royal
beliefs but convincing evidence to Fox that his hated rival was
the natural successor of Bute and North, '. . . the old system,
revived in the person of Lord Shelburne'.[5] By the end of
June, still not able to get the cabinet to take issue with
Shelburne, Fox had decided on resignation, though he had
not announced it by the time of Rockingham's death on 1
July, at which point Shelburne was already constructing his
own administration, forewarned of the Marquis's likely demise.

The Duke of Portland might be Rockingham's successor as
leader of the party but no one could deny the King his right
to choose the co-leader of the minister for the office of First
Lord. Few, even of the Rockingham group, would have
expected anyone other than Shelburne to be chosen. But Fox
had already decided not only that Shelburne should be
unmasked before he and the King destroyed ministry and
party, but that Fox himself would serve only under Portland
as First Lord, as he informed the King on 3 July. Fox's
resignation on Shelburne's appointment was followed by
those of Cavendish, Portland, Sheridan, Burke and several
other minor office-holders, though some of these were

reluctant martyrs and more were persuaded by Richmond to stay. At the time Fox's resignation was seen as pique and his argument that the cabinet should have chosen Rockingham's successor as administration leader because they represented the larger half of the administration was shocking, even to most Rockinghamites. Not for the first or last time Fox's reputation suffered a grievous blow.

But Shelburne's position was hardly stronger. Although Shelburne was the King's man and could convincingly pose as the defender of the constitution against the extravagant claims of party as expressed by Fox, and thus might rally the conservative majority to him, and although on America he quickly recognised the necessity of accepting unconditional independence, his ministry lacked personalities of first rank. William Pitt, at 23, was Chancellor of the Exchequer and had a great future, but no ministerial past. Like his chief he was seen by many as dangerously radical by virtue of his close association with Wyvill and parliamentary reform. Keppel remained at the Admiralty only until January, and he was not the only minister to leave. Nor was it only ministers Shelburne lacked. With North's followers numbering about 120 and Fox's about 90, Shelburne was short of heads, as well as good speakers in the House of Commons, the exact weakness of his position being hidden by the optimism of John Robinson. The attitude of independents could only be guessed at and Shelburne had the peace to push through Parliament. Above all Shelburne himself was the ministry's greatest liability. Pitt, who served under him, never employed him. Fox who could forgive North everything forgave Shelburne nothing. He was not trusted; domineering, apparently incapable of taking or asking for advice, he treated his colleagues as ciphers and rarely met them formally. 'You will certainly think the mode of keeping a cabinet unanimous by never meeting them at all an excellent one', wrote William Grenville, third son of George Grenville.[6]

The fate of his ministry was sealed by his failure to secure North's support. This he could not do without losing Keppel, Richmond, Grafton, Pitt and the outside support of Wyvill.

Worse, North was hostile to parliamentary reform which Shelburne could not abandon, but which Fox was prepared to lay aside for an alliance with North. The resignations of Keppel and Richmond, displeased by the peace preliminaries, in January 1783 eased the path to an alliance with North but left the ministry in tatters and the coalition could not occur until North saw the peace proposals.

Although, as we have seen, Shelburne had resisted any granting of independence to the colonies without concessions on the part of Congress, circumstances had quickly made such a position untenable. It would have proved impossible to re-open the war after Conway's motion for an end to the fighting against America of 27 February, which had led to North's resignation, and Parliament showed more concern about the need to resist the Bourbons than it did about the loss of the American colonies. By July Shelburne was also aware that his fall-back position of an offer of independence in return for some form of association with the colonies which would put an end to the alarming alliance of Congress with the Bourbons, was also receding rapidly from the realms of diplomatic possibility. He knew that Parliament would insist on security against France and Spain and protection for the interests of Loyalists. As the negotiations dragged on and Gibraltar barely withstood a Spanish siege, Shelburne could see little chance of progress.

But France and Spain were in dire financial straits and Franklin could foresee the Bourbons extricating themselves from the war against Britain and leaving the Americans in the lurch. By autumn Spanish failure against Gibraltar, French bankruptcy, American fears of losing fishing rights off the Atlantic coast and access to the lands to the west of the Appalachians – between the St Lawrence and Ohio rivers – as a result of a possible deal between France and Britain, to say nothing of the pressures on Shelburne, pushed all the participants towards a settlement.

Peace preliminaries were signed with Congress on 30 November. Unconditional recognition of American independence and American ownership of the western lands was accompanied by a promise that Congress would 'earnestly recommend' the separate states to indemnify and protect Loyalists. It was not a heroic peace but it was the best obtainable. Congress was willing to protect Loyalists, but the confederate nature of the American constitution, such as it was, gave it no authority in the matter.

Concessions were also made to France, though fewer than would have been extracted months earlier. Although George III and Shelburne would have conceded Gibraltar in return for reciprocal benefits, its stubborn defence had made it an object of patriotic pride. St Lucia, Senegal and Tobago, the restoration of St Pierre and Miquelon and the right to dry fish on the coasts of Newfoundland were the only French prizes, and Florida and Minorca the Spanish.

It was not a bad peace. The Bourbons and Americans each felt that the other had left them in the lurch; the territorial concessions to the Bourbons were minor and the agreement on the western lands would in Shelburne's view enable the Americans to expand, thus providing growing markets for British goods. But whether Parliament would be so sanguine was quite another matter, for the Loyalists had not been given any real security, while after Les Saintes and Gibraltar some might argue that the Bourbons had been too generously treated.

Lord North's attitude to the peace proposals would be crucial, but already the likelihood of his accepting them and of forging a coalition with Shelburne was slim. Shelburne could attract North only by accepting the loss of important supporters inside and outside Parliament. North's adamant opposition to reform was not the least of his objectionable qualities as far as Pitt and Wyvill were concerned. Moreover the collapse of the old relationship between the King and North made it unlikely that North would come to the rescue of George III's new favourite. North felt aggrieved that the King had left him with heavy debts as a result of the 1780 election, which North felt were the King's responsibility.

Courted by all, holding the balance in the Commons between, according to John Robinson's figures, Shelburne's 140 followers and Fox's 90 with his own 120, he awaited the peace preliminaries with interest, pressed by Robinson to accept them as the man who had lost the war, urged by William Eden to refuse them. Suspicious of Shelburne who was held back from making any firm offer to North by Pitt's intransigence, North turned to Fox and led the assault on the peace preliminaries in February, attacking the over-generous terms to France and America and what he chose to call the desertion of the Loyalists. The opposition majority was 224 votes to 208, but it is doubtful whether the peace preliminaries were what dictated men's votes. Each following held up well, loyalty to leader apparently meaning more than consideration of facts, an impression reinforced by the Fox–North coalition's subsequent reintroduction of the same peace proposals with a good majority.

In reality the War of Independence was a dead issue and the 'unprincipled' coalition of Fox and North had been secured days before the terms of the peace were laid before the House.

Thus, at last, the politicians were rid of the problem of the American colonies though not in the way that any would have wished. There had never been a fixed plan to suppress American liberties; there had been an understandable desire to find ways within the context of Empire of coping with imperial defence and a huge National Debt, pursued by politicians groping in a confused way to meet reasonable colonial demands in that context. American resistance to it was in the tradition of seventeenth-century resistance to what were seen as unconstitutional Crown demands and revolution was neither sought nor cheerfully embraced. Nonetheless the revolution in America saw the defeat and rejection of much of the *ancien régime* and the embracing of new concepts and systems not uninfluenced by the Enlightenment and in turn having an effect on revolutions in France and elsewhere. In that sense the successful war for independence seems to be an event of extraordinary importance. Britain also lost a colonial Empire and, partly, a war. It is important therefore to look at the impact of the war to see if it profoundly influenced the development of British politics and society.

EPILOGUE

America, the Old Regime and the Radical Challenge

The growth of radical activity and the development of a critique of the English constitution in the reign of George III is well enough attested, but the historian must be wary of assuming that because in 1832 the Parliamentary Reform Act was passed and because a tradition of radicalism can be traced for 70 years before then, the decline of the *ancien régime* was inevitable and its critics men of importance in the first twenty years of George III's reign. Indeed one might argue that the survival of the old regime, despite the blows it suffered between 1776 and 1783 is of a great deal more interest than its eventual collapse in quite different, and partly accidental, circumstances.

Despite the apparent solidity of Whig oligarchy between 1715 and 1760 it had always had many enemies. Popular Jacobitism probably absorbed much of the energy of those who found themselves outside the closed world of the political system until the 1750s and its demise was perhaps filled by 'Wilkes and Liberty' as a popular means of expressing dissent in a cheerful, but nonetheless strongly felt way. Nicholas Rogers has charted the existence of urban radicalism during the century and organised dissent was not inactive in this period.

The Tradition of 'Commonwealth', 'Old' or 'True' Whiggism never completely died in Britain and it was obviously vigorous in America. This Whiggism saw 1688 as an unfinished revolution which had failed to curb the authority of the Crown sufficiently when it had the chance, and had allowed the legislature to be tamed by corruption, a narrowing franchise and a standing army. Building on the work of opponents of royal power in the Civil War and Exclusion crisis – such men as Milton, Sidney, Harrington and Locke – in the early eighteenth century its ideas were carried on by Viscount Molesworth, John Trenchard and Thomas Gordon. They were not democrats but they did keep alive a tradition of resistance and dissent from the status quo, and, paradoxically, their ideas of executive hostility to legislative independence, and hence liberty, sounded a chord in Rockinghamite and Chathamite opposition to George III. Catherine Macaulay, sister of John Sawbridge, wrote a *History of England* produced over a period of twenty years from 1762, which developed this idea and helped to make it a strand of Whig historical orthodoxy.

Fears of executive power were also reflected in the closely allied 'country' tradition of opposition politics which flourished particularly under Walpole with Bolingbroke's assistance, but which remained the chief component of the ideology of parliamentary opposition until well into George III's reign. Seeking a remedy for the executive's overwhelming power in more frequent elections, an increase in the number of county seats, and in the passing of place and pensions bills, it strove to make Parliament not more representative but more independent. It appealed to oppositions as a means of securing co-operation between Whigs and Tories because it eschewed party issues and was common to both traditions. It could be, and was, at least in parts, acceptable to Rockinghamites, Chathamites and outside oppositions in George III's reign.

The new reign also saw a reawakening of dissent as a major element in radicalism after 40 years or more of a quiescence which it has always been difficult entirely to explain. The dissenting academies of the century produced men of considerable intellect and education and it would be quite impossible to imagine radicalism in eighteenth-century Britain without dissent. Dissenters, though tolerated and able to by-pass many of the restrictions imposed by the Clarendon Code and Test Act, were nonetheless not full citizens and still suffered from political and social disabilities. The Unitarian element in the blood-stream of many dissenting sects – and in some Anglicans such as Wyvill – though it had a limited number of adherents seems to have been particularly important in its rationalist approach not just to scripture but also to science and politics. Dr Price, James Burgh, John Jebb and Joseph Priestley were all Unitarians, and almost all radicals of any weight were dissenters or under unitarian influence.

Long before George III's accession, London had been a centre of criticism of Whig oligarchy and Court politics. Under Pelham the hostility felt in Walpole's time had been mitigated, but support for Pitt while he was seen as an enemy to oligarchy and friend to the merchant interest showed how that feeling of alienation remained. The peculiar constitution of the City and the large electorates of Middlesex, Southwark and Westminster ensured that London elected MPs hostile to the Court throughout the period. In George III's reign the mayoralties of Beckford (1762–3 and 1769–70), Townsend (1772–3), Sawbridge (1775–6) and Crosby (1770–71), to say nothing of Wilkes (1774–5), underline this continuing tradition. Rockinghamite failure to entrench a permanent party in the City under their preferred agent, the merchant Barlow Trecothick, and Chatham's uneasy relations with City politicians demonstrate the fact that London was alienated from not just politicians supported by the Court but from a political system dominated by aristocratic connections.

There is never a period when the development of communications and the press is not of fundamental importance to some individual historian, and we should therefore tread with caution. Nevertheless the growth in the number of London and provincial newspapers in the decades before George III's reign is remarkable and this growth continued unabated. By 1760 there were 40 provincial newspapers and between 1690 and 1780 the number of copies of newspapers printed annually rose from one million to fourteen million, a rate of increase far in excess of that of the population. Coffee houses, of which London possessed 550 by 1740, were centres at which dozens of men could read papers and discuss the news. Opposition papers predominated and it was Wilkes's and John Almon's use of the press in 1763 and 1768–9 which contributed so much to the national popularity of Wilkes, particularly in urban areas, which John Brewer has outlined in a number of articles.[1]

Given this background and the narrowness of the ruling élite by 1760, which John Cannon has demonstrated, it is difficult to imagine that some reawakened criticism of the political system would not have happened even without the impact of the quarrel with the colonists. Nor can we forget the impact of Wilkes, and it is perhaps best to yoke Wilkes and America together. After all, contemporaries saw parallels between the two issues. In America Wilkes was seen as a victim of the same malign forces as the colonists. 'Number 45' came to mean as much in America as it did in Britain. The legislature of South Carolina sent Wilkes £1500 and the New York Journal asserted that 'all Mr Wilkes's friends are friends of America'. Perhaps in order to replenish his depleted coffers, Wilkes was not slow to praise America for its love of liberty. The Society of Supporters of the Bill of Rights made the rights of the colonists equal with the rights of the Middlesex electors in its programme.

The Middlesex election and the taxation of the colonies together raised acutely the questions of 'no taxation without representation' and sovereignty as well as the argument that America was a testing ground for a policy of expanding the power of the Crown in Britain. In 1766 in *Reflexions on Representation* the author discussed the inequalities of the electoral system and urged a reform that would 'give every man . . . an influence in the publick deliberations proportional to his interest in them'.[2] Such a reform would base the vote on property but would demand a wider franchise and

wholesale redistribution of seats, especially to popular commercial boroughs. 'Every man in these Kingdoms is taxed,
that is a part of his property is taken from him; if this too is
done without his consent, which is taking also a part of his
liberty, in what sense can he be called free?'[3] Such an idea
was capable of a very democratic interpretation, and James
Burgh in *Political Disquisitions* (1774–5) pointed out that
almost all adults paid indirect taxes, and like Major Cartwright in *Take Your Choice* (1776) implied universal male
suffrage as the logical result. In such ways the arguments for
virtual representation already assailed by Otis were attacked
on the grounds of principle and logic. To Soame Jenyns'
defence of virtual representation at the time of the Stamp
Act controversy: 'Every Englishman is taxed, but not one in
twenty is [directly] represented',[4] Otis had made a reply
already stirring a response among certain elements in Britain. 'To what purpose is it to ring everlasting changes to
colonists in the cases of Manchester, Birmingham and
Sheffield, who return no members? If these now considerable places are not represented, they ought to be.'[5]

To the issue of representation was added that of
sovereignty. The question of the rights of electors, raised in
acute form by the Middlesex election, led easily to a discussion of where sovereignty ultimately lay. How were the rights
of electors to be protected if absolute power lay with King,
Lords and Commons? Indeed should power ultimately rest
anywhere? The American constitution of 1789 gave one
answer. Chatham never accepted the idea of parliamentary
sovereignty in full. Lord Camden, one of his most loyal
lieutenants, told the Lords: 'They cannot take away any
man's private property without making him a compensation'.
And later, he said, 'for whatever is a man's own, is absolutely
his own; no man hath a right to take it from him without his
consent, either expressed by himself or [his] representative'.[6]
Property rights were so much at the heart of eighteenth-
century belief in liberty that such an argument had force.
Expressions of doubt about Parliament's sovereignty had to
be expressed very cautiously in Parliament but outside such

ideas, not new to England, could be expressed more force-
fully.

John Brewer has argued that America, and Wilkes, did
have a profound effect on the development of radical
ideology.[7] Country attitudes were not abandoned but the
new elements in radical opposition now stressed parliamentary reform involving not just making Parliament more
independent but also more representative of property and
population. Chatham had expressed an interest in 1770. In
1774 Wilkes stressed the need for such reform and in 1776
recommended it to an indifferent House of Commons. The
Wyvill movement, the Duke of Richmond and Pitt the
Younger all took up the demand for parliamentary reform.
John Brewer has argued that America strengthened the case
for reform and acted as its 'ideological mid-wife'.[8] It highlighted the defects in the political system and, once shown
up, these defects would never be entirely forgotten.

Nor was the impact of Wilkes and America purely ideological. The petitioning movement for the repeal of the Stamp
Act and, even more, that of 1769 initiated a mode of public
pressure which would be used time and time again by radical
movements. The ideas put forward by James Burgh in his
Political Disquisitions of 1774–5 for a national association of
men of property to press for reform by petitioning, and John
Jebb's ideas for extending Wyvill's Association Movement
into a rival electoral system and national assembly, not only
echoed what radicals did in America but became part of
radical pressure tactics ever after. Wilkes and America
spawned the Society of Supporters of the Bill of Rights
(1769), a generally radical body dedicated to reform and
committed to a programme of specific policies. Out of Wilkes
and America and the ferment of reform came the Society for
Constitutional Information (1780), itself a by-product of
Wyvill's movement. Largely a propaganda organisation it
sought to disseminate information and propaganda to 'the
community at large ... through every village and hamlet'.
Led by Cartwright, Jebb, Capel Lofft and with a membership
of MPs, aldermen and professional men it was no revolution-

ary organisation. But its aims were democratic and although its membership was élitist, it had a profound effect on the radical politics of the age of the French Revolution. Finally the moral effect of a successful act of resistance to authority and of a rejection of many of the assumptions about the traditional bases of political power cannot have been insignificant.

And yet it is too easy to allow ourselves to be carried away by all this. The membership of the SCI was only 130 strong. The number of committed radicals was small; the same names crop up time and time again: Sawbridge, Townsend, the Reverend John Horne, Jebb, Burgh, Lofft, Cartwright. Although significant in the history of radicalism such men are, like the radicals of our own time, in several organisations at once, professional progressives. And even if these men are, as they certainly must be, significant within the history of radicals, that does not make radicalism necessarily significant in British Politics at the time. Economical reforms were passed by the Rockinghams but they owed nothing to Wyvill or other radicals. When Pitt, Wyvill's ally, became First Lord in 1784 he could not pass parliamentary reform. The King was hostile and the House of Commons showed even less sympathy for the idea in 1785 than it had in 1780, despite the fact that Pitt had watered down his proposals and despite the conservative, country-party nature of the franchise and redistribution proposals. Radicalism itself seemed to go into eclipse between the fall of North and the rise of the movement for the Repeal of the Test and Corporation Acts after 1787. While that movement owed a great deal to the efforts of radicals in the 1770s and while the impact of the French Revolution was to renew and magnify the radical efforts of the earlier decade the events of the 1790s show just how vigorous the old regime still was; vigorous and acceptable to most Englishmen.

For George III's Britain in the 1780s was still a society dominated by aristocracy and gentry. 'The Industrial Revolution' had hardly started and although some towns were growing rapidly and might feel that recognition of their status was overdue, only four cities had shown any desire to join Wyvill's plan of association in 1780, and there was just as little visible support for parliamentary reform. The most obvious thing about radicalism in the 1790s is its unpopularity and ineffectiveness compared with the conservatism, not only of the ruling elements, but of the wider population. While it may be true that America stimulated new vigour and new direction in radicalism it also invigorated conservative attitudes. Samuel Johnson's series of pamphlets in the 1770s, culminating in the very specific *Taxation No Tyranny* of 1775, warned that if the 'fabric of subordination' is destroyed then 'society is dissolved into a tumult of individuals' and his ideas were given reinforcement and authority by John Wesley, who characterised himself as 'one that believes God, not the people, to be the origin of all civil power' and warned his followers, and anyone else who would listen, against 'designing men' determined to overthrow government in America and England, urging them instead to fear God and honour the King.[9]

Although America might have acted as ideological midwife to new radical ideas it is worth pointing out that the radicalism of Burgh, Price and Priestley was rooted in an English past as much as in an American present. Burgh's *Disquisitions* owed most to the Commonwealth Whig tradition. And such a revival of radical ideas provoked a vigorous conservative defence of the constitution. 'This doctrine of universal representation utterly overthrows the present happy constitution of Great Britain, destroys all order, degree and subordination in the state and makes the fabric of society a ruin and a heap of rubbish', wrote an anonymous author in the *Public Advertiser* of 1766. Burke complained over a decade later of the Methodists' addiction to the 'slavish doctrines of Charles the 2nd's reign', but the reaction against the Americans' ideas and their English radical supporters was particularly fierce among the nobility and gentry who stood most to lose from their more general application.

While Paine in *Common Sense* (1776) convinced Americans that monarchy was neither rooted in divine institution nor utility and paved the way for the radicalism of the 1780s and 1790s, his ideas seemed shocking in England. Dr Price noted with alarm the revival of the idea that 'there are some of mankind who are born with an inherent right of dominion'.[10] It is surprising that he should imagine that the idea had ever gone away, but it is no doubt the case that when America seemed to challenge the patriarchal view of society that society reasserted its principles anew. The battle lines of Church and King on one side and Dissent and Popular Sovereignty on the other, familiar in the 1790s, were already being drawn.

In the early 1780s, despite the loss of the American colonies, a loss potentially disturbing to social quiet, the remarkable fact is that after some ineffective reforms and Dunning's generalised motion of discontent, little happened. North's fall was almost enough and the emergence of the independent Pitt to high office seemed to obviate the need for radical change. Wyvill's movement slowly declined towards dissolution in 1785. Pitt failed to carry parliamentary reform. Society and Parliament were still dominated by aristocracy and gentry. Respect was still genuinely paid to the ancient constitution and to its head, the King. In January 1784 Humphrey Sibthorp, MP for Boston in Lincolnshire, wrote to his friend John Strutt, 'I am, I freely own it, not so much any man's friend as I am the King's nor do I wish in these times to purge off all Tory blood'.[11] This did not prevent his disapproval of the King's intervention against Fox's India Bill, but his criticism of the King's action was clearly for conservative reasons, that is royal interference in the deliberations of the House of Lords, just as many an independent's support for the King over India arose from that same conservatism. It would have taken a great deal to pierce the belief in the fundamental virtues of the British constitution and in the social hierarchy it protected, a great deal more weight than a handful of radicals could provide.

Public opinion still counted for little. The press was an extensive and effective means of communication between ruling and ruled but it did not manipulate public opinion or influence the political nation to do anything which it was not disposed to do. Political power remained firmly in the hands of the landed élite and it had no sympathy for reform of a radical kind. Pitt found to his cost, as had his father, Beckford and Townsend in 1768, that parliamentary reform was largely a metropolitan interest. Economical reform occurred because it suited the Rockinghams and they, for a time, had power. Reform of franchise, redistribution, any challenge to sovereignty of Parliament or to the ancient constitution met with short shrift from those who expected to suffer from them. Such public opinion as we can detect outside London and a few counties like Yorkshire and Middlesex blamed defeat in America on bad ministers not on the constitution itself, or at the most detected a need for a little readjustment to the balance of that constitution.

So the political system emerged from the loss of the American colonies remarkably unscathed. George III's victory over the Fox–North coalition was only two years after his forced relinquishing of his favourite minister. In 1789 George III celebrated his recovery from illness in a City which cheered him and his ministers to the echo. The demands of dissenters for the repeal of the Test and Corporation Acts would reveal the deep-rooted conservatism of Englishmen. The *ancien régime* might have suffered a mortal blow in America but kingly and oligarchic rule in Britain survived bruised but not suffering any serious injury.

NOTES

INTRODUCTION

1. J. R. Pole, *Political Representation in England and the Origins of the American Republic* (London, 1966); Pauline Maier, *From Resistance to Revolution* (London, 1973); L. H. Gipson, *The Coming of Revolution 1763–1775* (New York, 1954).
2. Pauline Maier, op. cit.
3. 'Every man in England seems to consider himself as a piece of sovereign over America', Franklin Papers, xiv, 65.

1. ORIGINS AND PURPOSES

1. James Henretta, *Salutary Neglect: Colonial Administration under the Duke of Newcastle* (Princeton, 1972).
2. Dora Mae Clark, *The Rise of the British Treasury* (Yale, 1960).
3. Newcastle to Board of Trade, 24 October 1727, State Papers, quoted in Henretta, op. cit.
4. Quoted in Edmund and Helen Morgan, *The Stamp Act Crisis: Prologue to Revolution* (New York, 1963).
5. Quoted in Henretta, op. cit., p. 77.
6. Quoted in Henretta, op. cit., p. 103, and Albert B. Southwick, 'The Molasses Act – Source of Precedents', *William and Mary Quarterly* (July, 1951).
7. Governor James Glen to the Duke of Bedford, Secretary of State for the South, 1748, quoted in Henretta, op. cit., p. 244.
8. Works of John Adams, II, pp. 521–523, quoted in L. H. Gipson, op. cit., pp. 37–8.

9. Franklin Papers, xiii, p. 522, quoted in P. D. G. Thomas, *British Politics and the Stamp Act Crisis* (Oxford, 1975) p. 26.
10. Allen–Chew Correspondence, quoted in P. D. G. Thomas, op. cit., p. 24.
11. I. R. Christie, *Crisis of Empire* (London, 1966) p. 22.
12. The size of the Court party is discussed in 'The Political Management of Sir Robert Walpole 1720–1742' by Eveline Cruickshanks in *Britain in the Age of Walpole*, edited by Jeremy Black (London, 1984). Also in A. S. Foord, *His Majesty's Opposition* (Oxford, 1964) and B. W. Hill, *The Growth of Parliamentary Parties 1689–1742* (London, 1976).
13. J. P. Kenyon, *Revolution Principles – The Politics of Party 1689–1720* (Cambridge, 1977).
14. Quoted in H. T. Dickinson, *Liberty and Property* (London, 1977), pp. 141–2.
15. Ibid., p. 146.
16. Ibid., p. 154.
17. Parl. Hist., xv, p. 744.
18. John Cannon, *Parliamentary Reform 1640–1832* (Cambridge, 1972).
19. John Cannon, *Aristocratic Century: The Peerage of Eighteenth Century England* (Cambridge, 1974).
20. J. C. D. Clark, *English Society 1688–1832* (Cambridge, 1985).
21. Newcastle's own notes, BM Add MSS 33001, f. 83, quoted in Henretta, op. cit., p. 341.
22. Hardwicke to Newcastle, 1753, Add MSS 32736, ff. 340–343, quoted in Henretta, op. cit., p. 341.
23. Henretta, op. cit., chap. 7, p. 324 ff.
24. Bernard Bailyn, *Ideological Origins of the American Revolution* (Cambridge, Mass., 1967).
25. Paul Langford, 'William Pitt and Public Opinion, 1757', *English Historical Review*, 1973.
26. Linda Colley, *In Defiance of Oligarchy, The Tory Party 1714–60* (Cambridge, 1982).
27. Eveline Cruickshanks, *Political Untouchables, The Tories and the '45* (London, 1979); J. C. D. Clark, *The Dynamics of Change* (Cambridge, 1982).
28. 'Votes and Proceedings of the Pennsylvania Assembly', cited in Alan Rogers, *Empire and Liberty* (California, 1974).
29. 'Pennsylvania Assembly to the Governor', cited in Rogers, op. cit., p. 103.
30. Quoted in J. C. Long, *Lord Jeffrey Amherst, King's Soldier* and cited by Rogers, op. cit., p. 63.

31. John L. Bullion, *A Great and Necessary Measure. George Grenville and the Genesis of the Stamp Act* (Missouri, 1982), quoting the Liverpool papers.

2. PRINCIPLE AND PRAGMATISM

1. *Letters from George III to Lord Bute 1756–66* (ed.) Romney Sedgewick (London, 1939).
2. Thomas Whateley: 'The regulations lately made concerning the colonies . . .' quoted in John L. Bullion, op. cit., p. 48.
3. Thomas Whately: 'Considerations on the trade and finances of this Kingdom . . .', 1765, quoted in John L. Bullion, op. cit., p. 48.
4. Petition of New York Assembly to Parliament, October 1765.
5. According to John L. Bullion this argument is that of Charles Jenkinson (Appendix C to *A Great and Necessary Measure*).
6. Thomas Whately: 'Mr Secretary Whateley's General Plan', 1764, cited in Bullion, op. cit.
7. George Grenville in House of Commons, 6 February 1765, *Parliamentary Diaries of Nathaniel Ryder 1764–67*, Camden Series.
8. Horace Walpole, *Memoirs*.
9. John Brooke, *King George III*.
10. *Letters of Philip Dormer Fourth Earl of Chesterfield* (ed.) B. Dobrée, 17 August 1765, quoted in Paul Langford, *The First Rockingham Administration* (Oxford, 1973).
11. Hardwicke, *Private Memoirs*, Add MS 35428, f. 27, quoted in Langford, op. cit.
12. Cited in Langford, op. cit., p. 26.
13. Duke of Bedford quoted in Ross J. S. Hoffman, *The Marquis* (New York (Fordham), 1973).
14. In Georgia the Governor secured compliance with the Act, but even here only temporarily.
15. Horace Walpole, *Memoirs*.
16. Duke of Newcastle to Rockingham, 12 October 1765.
17. Fitzwilliam Papers, Conway to Colonial Governors and General Gage, quoted in Langford, op. cit.
18. Rockingham Memorandum, cited in P. D. G. Thomas, op. cit.
19. George Grenville, cited in Langford, op. cit., p. 212.
20. Edmund Burke, First Conciliation Proposals 1775.
21. Horace Walpole, *Memoirs*.
22. Sir Edward Turner, MP for Penryn and a supporter of

Grenville, quoted in Langford, op. cit., p. 155.

23. Edmund Burke, *Thoughts on the Causes of the Present Discontents*, 1770.

24. John Hobart, second Earl, quoted in John Brooke, op. cit.

25. James Harris, MP for Christchurch; a friend of Grenville.

26. Charles Townshend, House of Commons 1767; quoted in Sir Lewis Namier and John Brooke, *Charles Townshend*, 1964.

27. William Johnson, agent for Connecticut; quoted in P. D. G. Thomas, op. cit., p. 350.

28. Charles Pratt, first Earl of Camden, an opponent of the Declaratory Act, a Pittite, to the Duke of Grafton; cited by I. R. Christie and B. W. Laboree, *Empire or Independence*.

29. Ibid.

30. Franklin Papers.

31. Samuel Adams to Peter Timothy in *The Writings of Samuel Adams* (New York, 1904–8); quoted in Maier, op. cit.

32. Grenville Papers.

33. *Correspondence of King George III* (ed.) Sir J. Fortescue.

34. The Hon. John Yorke to his father, Philip Yorke, Earl of Hardwicke, quoted in Langford, op. cit.

35. Quoted in Stanley Ayling, *The Elder Pitt*.

36. A very useful guide to this subject is P. J. Marshall, *Problems of Empire 1757–1813* (London, 1968).

37. John Cannon, op. cit; J. V. Beckett, *The Aristocracy in England* (Oxford: Blackwells, 1986); L. & J. C. F. Stone, *An Open Elite? England 1540–1880* (Oxford, 1984).

38. Jeremy Black's *The English Press in the Eighteenth Century*, 1987, is the best account of the subject.

3.   LORD NORTH AND THE LOSS OF THE AMERICAN COLONIES

1. Journal of the House of Burgesses, cited in Gipson, op. cit.

2. Dartmouth to Governor Hutchinson April 1773, quoted in B. Donoughue, *British Politics and the American Revolution 1773–75*, London 1964.

3. Cabinet Minute 29 January 1774, quoted in Donoughue, op. cit., p. 34.

4. Donoughue, op. cit.

5. George III to Lord North March 1774, *Letters of King George III* (ed.) Sir J. Fortescue, quoted in Donoughue, op. cit.

6. Burke to New York Assembly Committee of Correspondence

April 1774, cited in Donoughue, op. cit., p. 83.

7. Franklin to Speaker of Massachusetts House of Representatives March 1774.

8. Parliamentary History of England, cited in Donoughue, op. cit.

9. North to Governor Hutchinson November 1774 and George III to North November 1774, *Letters of George III* (ed.) Fortescue.

10. Cited in Bernard Bailyn, op. cit.

11. Ibid.

12. Daniel A. Baugh, 'Why did Britain lose command of the sea during the war for America?' in *The British Navy and the Use of Naval Power in the Eighteenth Century*, eds. Jeremy Black and Philip Woodfine (Leicester, 1988).

13. P. R. O. Rodney to his son, 7 March 1781. I am grateful to Dr R. J. B. Knight of the National Maritime Museum for permission to quote from his paper on Sandwich, '"Some farther degree of merit": The fall and rise of the reputation of Lord Sandwich'.

14. *Letters of Horace Walpole.*

15. R. Arthur Bowler, *Logistics and the Failure of the British Army in America 1775–1783* (Princeton, 1975).

16. Cited in Donoughue, op. cit., p. 98.

17. Cited by Dr R. J. B. Knight in his paper on Sandwich (see note 13 above).

18. Richard Middleton, *The Bells of Victory* (Cambridge, 1985).

19. Lord North to George III in *Correspondence of King George III* (ed.) Fortescue.

20. Cited in P. D. G. Thomas, *Lord North*, p. 125.

21. George III to Lord North, *Correspondence of King George III* (ed.) Fortescue.

22. Ibid.

23. Ibid.

4.   THE FAILURE OF OPPOSITION

1. Burke's conciliation proposals 1775.

2. Edmund Burke to Rockingham 1775, cited in Donoughue, op. cit., p. 129.

3. Josiah Tucker, 'A Letter to Edmund Burke 1775', quoted in G. H. Guttridge, *English Whiggism and the American Revolution* (University of California, 1966).

4. Quoted in Lewis Namier, *England in the Age of the American Revolution*, London 1930, p. 255.
5. Elizabeth Boody Schumpeter, *English Overseas Trade Statistics 1697–1808* (Oxford, 1960).
6. William Lee to Thomas Adams March 1775, quoted in Donoughue, op. cit., p. 156 n.i; and Namier, op. cit., p. 255.
7. Burke to Rockingham August 1775, quoted in Donoughue, op. cit., p. 156.
8. Fox to Rockingham, *Fox's Memoirs* Vol. I.

5. ROCKINGHAM, SHELBURNE AND PEACE-MAKING

1. John Norris, *Shelburne and Reform* (London, 1963); I. R. Christie, *Wilkes, Wyvill and Reform* (London, 1962); John Cannon, op. cit.; J. Ehrman, *The Younger Pitt: The Years of Acclaim* (London, 1969).
2. *Letters of King George III* (ed.) Fortescue.
3. *Memorials and Correspondence of Charles James Fox* (ed.) Lord John Russell, quoted in John Cannon, *The Fox North Coalition* (Cambridge, 1969), p. 5.
4. The whole question of the effectiveness of the Rockinghamite Economical Reform measures is discussed in I. R. Christie, 'Economical Reform and the Influence of the Crown', *Cambridge Historical Journal*, 1956; A. S. Foord, 'The Waning of the Influence of the Crown', *English Historical Review*, 1947; B. Kemp, 'Crewe's Act, 1782', *English Historical Review*, 1953.
5. *Memorials and Correspondence* . . . (ed.) Lord John Russell.
6. Cited in John Cannon, op. cit., p. 37.

EPILOGUE

1. 'Commercialisation and Politics' in *The Birth of a Consumer Society* by Neil McKendrick, John Brewer and J. A. Plumb (London, 1982); in *Party Ideology and Popular Politics at the Accession of George III*, and in *An Ungovernable People* by John Brewer and John Styles.
2. 'Reflexions on Representation in Parliament . . .', 1766, quoted in John Brewer, *Party Ideology and Popular Politics at the Accession of George III* (Cambridge, 1977), p. 213.
3. Ibid.
4. 'The objections to the taxation of our American colonies . . . briefly considered.'

5. *Boston Gazette*, July 1765.
6. House of Lords 10 February 1766, *Parliamentary History of England*, Vol. XVI.
7. John Brewer, op. cit.
8. Ibid.
9. John Wesley's opinions on America are discussed by J. C. D. Clark in *English Society 1688–1832* (Cambridge, 1989).
10. The variety of English reactions to the American Revolution, including those of Burke and Dr Price, are discussed in J. C. D. Clark, op. cit.
11. A letter to John Strutt, January 1784, cited in Sir Lewis Namier and John Brooke, *The House of Commons 1754–1790*, Vol. III (London, 1961).

FURTHER READING

The number of books published on the subject of British politics and the American Revolution is enormous and what follows is merely a personal selection, but nearly all the works mentioned contain extensive bibliographies to guide the student through further study.

There are many excellent general surveys. Those by British historians include I. R. Christie's *Crisis of Empire*, a masterly digest with a good bibliography, while Peter Wells's *The American War of Independence* is a very clear and concise survey of the main issues. Among many useful American contributions are J. R. Alden's *Britain and the Loss of the American Colonies*, though its author is not able to shake off a considerable degree of Whig prejudice, J. C. Miller's *Origins of the American Revolution*, and L. H. Gipson's masterly *The Coming of the Revolution*. Christie and B. W. Laboree collaborated on an Anglo–American double view of the crisis in *Empire and Independence* which usefully shows different national perspectives on the same events.

Anglo–American relations before 1763 are well served by excellent studies. The role of the Treasury in contributing to independence is dealt with by Dora Mae Clark in *The Rise of the Treasury* and J. A. Henretta's *Salutary Neglect*. Ideological differences between Britain and America are well covered in Bernard Bailyn's *The Ideological Origins of the American Revolution* and his *The Origins of American Politics* and by Caroline Robbins's *The Eighteenth Century Commonwealth Man* and J. R. Pole's *Political Representation in England and the Origins of the American Republic*. H. T. Dickinson's *Liberty and Property* is an excellent survey of British political ideas, though it

135

seriously underestimates the survival of Toryism. *Aristocratic Century* and *Parliamentary Reform, 1640–1832*, both by John Cannon, are invaluable surveys of oligarchic society and its critics in Britain. Richard Hofstadter's *America in 1750* and L. H. Gipson's monumental *The British Empire before the American Revolution* are important guides to a crucial topic and Alan Rogers' *Empire and Liberty* underlines the strains put on relations between Britain and the thirteen colonies by the Seven Years' War.

The subject of British politics 1754–1783 has produced many good books but there remain serious gaps. I. R. Christie's *Wars and Revolution* is sound and John Derry's *English Politics and the American Revolution* is sensible and sharp. George III is well served by two biographers, John Brooke and Stanley Ayling. Richard Pares' *King George III and the Politicians* remains a gold mine, and equally exciting is John Brewer's *Party Ideology and Popular Politics at the Accession of George III*.

The ministers who served the King have been patchily served by historians. Bute is best studied in Namier, in Karl W. Schweizer's *Lord Bute: Essays in Reinterpretation* or in the biographies of the King. George Grenville now has a *Political Biography* by Philip Lawson which is very welcome and his administration's American policy is covered by John L. Bullion's *A Great and Necessary Measure: The Genesis of the Stamp Act* and P. D. G. Thomas's very fine *British Politics and the Stamp Act*, which is required reading not only for Grenville but also for the subsequent events of Rockingham's and Chatham's administrations. Ross J. S. Hoffmann has written a useful biography of Rockingham called *The Marquis* and it can be supplemented by Paul Langford's *The First Rockingham Administration* and Frank O'Gorman's indispensable *The Rise of Party in England* which covers the Rockingham party's fortunes and its relations with other groups from 1760 to 1783. Also useful in this context are O'Gorman's short but detailed *Rise of the Two Party System* and B. W. Hill's *British Parliamentary Parties 1742–1832*. G. H. Guttridge's *English Whiggism and the American Revolution* needs to be read in conjunction with I. R. Christie's essay 'Was There a New Toryism?', printed in his book of essays, *Myth and Reality*.

Chatham remains a controversial and remote figure. The great biography by Basil Williams does not manage entirely to avoid hagiography and recent biographies by Peter Brown and Stanley Ayling have helped to redress the balance. Essential reading is John Brooke's *The Chatham Administration; 1766–1768* and also very useful are John Norris's *Shelburne*, Peter Brown's *The Chathamites* and D. A. Winstanley's *Lord Chatham and the Whig Opposition*, though much of it has been overtaken by the work of O'Gorman and Hill.

Lord North cannot be better studied than in the pages of P. D. G. Thomas's succinct biography. *British Politics and the American Revolution 1773–1775* by B. Donoughue is a detailed study of government and opposition reactions to the crisis of these years. The standard work on North's fall is Christie's *The End of Lord North's Ministry*. The Fox–North coalition and the history of subsequent administrations to 1783 are covered in the uniformly satisfying *The Fox–North Coalition* by John Cannon, *C. J. Fox and the Disintegration of the Whig Party* by L. G. Mitchell and John Ehrman's *The Younger Pitt; The Years of Acclaim*.

The impact of America on the development of radicalism in Britain is best covered in general terms by John Cannon's *Parliamentary Reform*, E. Royle and J. Walvin's *English Radicals and Reformers* and C. Bonwick's *English Radicals and the American Revolution*. The relationship with the Wilkes and Wyvill movements is touched on in G. Rudé's *Wilkes and Liberty* and I. R. Christie's excellent *Wilkes, Wyvill and Reform*. The development of radical ideology is best dealt with in H. T. Dickinson's *Liberty and Property* and the general background of social unrest is illuminated by W. J. Shelton's *English Hunger and Industrial Disorders* and J. Stevenson's *Popular Disturbances in England 1700–1870*.

The 'revisionist' school of eighteenth-century British historians has yet to get its teeth into the American Revolution but J. C. D. Clark's two works, *English Society 1688–1832* and *Revolution and Rebellion* have already modified views on the impact of America on the growth of radical ideas by inference. Although the book is concerned with the impact of the French, rather than the American, Revolution on British society, I. R. Christie's *Stress and Stability* underlines the features of English society and administration which made for stability and a strong conservative sentiment.

The war itself is a vast subject. Readers will find John Selby's *The Road to Yorktown* excellent. Piers Mackesy's *The War for America* is essential reading as is R. Arthur Bowler's *Logistics and the Failure of the British Army in America 1775–1783*. Lord George Germain has a good biographer in Alan Valentine but an unprejudiced and modern biography of Sandwich is needed. There are excellent essays by Daniel A. Baugh, David Syrett and Kenneth Breen in *The British Navy and the Use of Naval Power in the Eighteenth Century*, edited by Jeremy Black and Philip Woodfine.

Finally, the following works will be found helpful: Dora Mae

Clark's *British Opinion and the American Revolution*, M. G. Kammen's *A Rope of Sand; The Colonial Agents, British Politics and the American Revolution*, F. B. Wickwire's *British Subministers and Colonial America 1763–1781* and J. C. Sainty's *Treasury Officials 1660–1870*.

APPENDIX I: DRAMATIS PERSONAE, 1754–84

Where the character's career is sufficiently covered in the text I have avoided repeating facts.

Adams: John (1735–1826) Vice-President of the United States under Washington; President 1797–1801. A Massachusetts lawyer, he came into prominence and active politics in the Stamp Act crisis. His move to Boston and friendship with James Otis and John Hancock increased his involvement but he was a cautious Whig, opposed to mob rule and fearful of the possible consequences of independence. Organised the defence of the guards involved in the Boston Massacre, sat in all the Continental Congresses, helped draft the Declaration of Independence once convinced of its inevitability and took a leading part in the peace negotiations of 1781–3.

Adams: Sam (1722–1803) Rose to prominence with the Stamp Act agitation and sank into relative insignificance once the war began. Mentioned in John Adams's diary for 1763 as a member of the Caucus Club, centre of opposition to Governor Bernard and Lieutenant-Governor Hutchinson with the latter of whom Adams had a personal quarrel. A brilliant agitator, he helped secure the radical majority in the Massachusetts House of Representatives in 1766 and became its leader. He orchestrated the radical campaign against the Townshend duties, largely created the Sons of Liberty and inter-colonial committees of correspondence, and kept the radical flame alive between 1770 and 1774. A vociferous proponent of independence in the Second Continental Congress, he showed little ability for constructive politics after 1776.

Barré: Colonel Isaac (1726–1802) MP for Chipping Wycombe (1761–74) and Calne (1774–90), he served at Quebec as Adjutant-General to Wolfe and was brought into Parliament by Shelburne. Losing all his military appointments after attacking Grenville in 1763, he opposed the Stamp Act, always keeping in close contact with American friends. Refusing office under Rockingham he accepted it under Chatham, resigning with his patron Shelburne in 1768. He opposed the war but sought to find ways to keep links with the colonies. In Parliament he suffered from a debating style that was abusive and threatening.

Barrington: William Wildman (1717–93) second Viscount MP for Berwick (1748–54), Plymouth (1754–78). A loyal supporter of government, not a party man. Secretary of War (1755–61 and 1765–78), he held other offices also between 1746 and 1782. A good speaker and useful to government. Increasingly unhappy with North's government after 1774, he left the House of Commons for the Lords in 1778.

Beckford: William (1709–70) MP for Shaftesbury (1747–54), London (1754–70). Landowner, merchant, plantation owner, originally a Jacobite Tory, he declared himself a Whig in 1763 and became an enthusiastic Pittite and City radical. Lord Mayor of London (1762–63), he disliked and resented Wilkes and was never a member of the Society of the Supporters of the Bill of Rights.

Bedford: John Russell (1710–71) fourth Duke of Opponent of Sir Robert Walpole and supporter of Lord Carteret, he accepted office under Henry Pelham (1744) as First Lord of the Admiralty. Secretary of State for the South (1748–51). In opposition, an ally of Cumberland and Fox. Lord Lieutenant of Ireland (1756–61) and ambassador for the peace negotiations with France in 1762. Quarrelling with Bute he joined Grenville's ministry, offending the King, particularly over the Regency Bill. Dismissed in 1765 he joined Grafton's administration in 1767 after failing to come to terms with Rockingham in opposition. Blindness ended his political career. He and his followers remained committed to the principles of the Stamp Act.

Burgh: James (1714–75) Author of *Political Disquisitions* (1774–75), a book whose ideas on representation and taxation showed him to be a radical far ahead of his time. Wrote articles in favour of annual Parliaments, manhood suffrage, place bills and the rights of the American colonists. His ideas for an Association to petition and press for reform passed into the tactical armoury of radicalism.

Burgoyne: John (1723–92) General MP for Midhurst (1761–68), Preston (1768–92). Gave distinguished service in the Seven Years' War. On American policy he opposed repeal of Stamp Act, and supported the Declaratory Act. He secured royal favour though not always voting with the Court and, despite quarrelling with North, supported American policy. Saratoga ended his military career and he opposed North and Germain in Parliament. Rockingham made him commander in Ireland.

Burke: Edmund (1729–97) MP for various constituencies (1765–94). Achieved no high office and is renowned chiefly for his political writings, especially during the French Revolution. Private secretary and adviser to Rockingham he developed the idea of 'party' in *Thoughts on the Cause of the Present Discontents*. On America he was perceptive about the likely consequences of Townshend's duties but his belief that, although Parliament had rights in America, particularly those of taxation, it was not always expedient for a parent to exercise his rights over his children, was unlikely to make much headway in such a patriarchal society and his schemes for conciliation were not acceptable in Britain or America.

Bute: John Stuart (1713–93) third Earl of A Scottish representative peer (1737–41), he took little part in public affairs until re-elected in 1761. Rose through favour with Frederick, Prince of Wales, and Princess Augusta, and as mentor to the future George III. Political adviser to Princess Augusta after Frederick's death in 1751, he helped negotiate the settlement of 1757 between Newcastle and Pitt but by 1760 was disgusted with both. The new reign saw him established as the feared favourite: Privy Councillor and Groom of the Stole (1760); Secretary for the North (1761), and First Lord of the Treasury (1762). He won the hostility of a generation of politicians and, although by 1765 his relationship with the King was a thing of the past, it continued to overshadow and distort the political relationships of the reign for some considerable time.

Cartwright: John (1740–1824) Of old gentry stock but educated at a dissenter academy, he began his career in the navy and was an enthusiast for naval efficiency, but his chief fame is as a political radical. An enthusiast for American independence, advocate of annual Parliaments, universal suffrage and the ballot, he was a member of the Westminster Association (1780) and founder of the fount of radical personnel and ideas, the Society for Constitutional Information (1780). His radical career continued into the time of Peterloo.

Chatham: first Earl of   (see Pitt the Elder)

Conway: Henry Seymour (1717–95) Field Marshal   Irish and later a Westminster MP (1741–56). Opposed Grenville's government and was dismissed from his civilian and military posts. Was Secretary of State for Rockingham and an inadequate Leader of the House. Served under Pitt, though unhappy at continued Rockinghamite exclusion, but continued until Bedford joined the ministry when he gave up all offices, remaining in the cabinet until 1770. Opposed the Massachusetts Bay Regulating Act and condemned the war. Commander-in-Chief (1782–83) but his opposition to Pitt lost him his seat in 1784.

Dartmouth: William Legge (1731–1801) second Earl of   Stepbrother to Lord North. President of Board of Trade under Rockingham, resigning on the formation of Chatham's ministry. Secretary of State for the American Colonies in 1772 on Hillsborough's resignation. Though anxious for conciliation with America he advised rejection of the Olive Branch petition. He moved to the office of Lord Privy Seal (1775–82), happy to escape responsibility for coercion of the colonists.

Dickinson: John (1732–1808)   Born in Maryland, he studied law in London and practised in Philadelphia which he represented in the Pennsylvanian legislature (1762–64) where he was Benjamin Franklin's leading conservative opponent and as such failed to secure re-election until 1770. He opposed the Stamp Act and was a leading member of the Stamp Act Congress. His *Farmer's Letters* brought him fame and helped create the united opposition to Townshend's duties, but he was no radical and detested the tactics and aims of such as Sam Adams. He withdrew from the first Continental Congress but still drafted its petition to George III. He opposed the Declaration of Independence and wrote the Olive

Branch Petition. He nonetheless fought during the war and had a distinguished career after 1783.

Dowdeswell: William (1721–75)   MP for Tewkesbury and, later, Worcester (1747–53), (1761–75). Sat originally as a Tory, particularly keen to see a reduction in the army and taxes. Opposed the Stamp Act and the use of General Warrants but grew to fame chiefly through opposition to the Cider Excise (1763). His selection as Chancellor of the Exchequer by Rockingham was a surprise but he was a leading adviser, particularly on the Declaratory Act and America from 1766.

Dunning: John (1731–83)   MP for Shelburne's borough of Calne (1768–82). A formidable advocate and speaker in the Commons. His friendship with Camden brought him to Shelburne's notice and he was made Solicitor-General in 1768, staying in the post for a year after the resignations from office of Chatham and Shelburne. He took the lead in Parliament in the movement to reduce the supposedly growing influence of the Crown, culminating in his resolutions of 1780. Entered the House of Lords in 1783.

Fox: Charles James (1749–1806)   MP for various constituencies (1768–1806). The second son of Henry Fox, Lord of the Admiralty (1770–72); Lord of the Treasury (1773–74); Secretary of State for Foreign Affairs (1782) and again in 1783 and 1806. Voted with government at first and was rewarded with place in 1770, but his indolence, rakish reputation and above all his opposition to the Royal Marriages Bill, plus his inveterate hatred of the King led to his dismissal in 1774. He drifted into an alliance with the Rockinghams, filial piety forbidding connection with Shelburne or Chatham. He opposed most of the Intolerable Acts and soon became the leading opposition spokesman in the Commons. The events of 1782–4 were to keep him out of office for over twenty years.

Fox: Henry (1705–74)   MP (1735–63), created Baron Holland (1763). Almost never without office (1737–63) but despite his connections and skills as a debater and parliamentary manager he held high office only briefly (1755–56 and 1762–63). Thought of as cynical and avaricious, he was closely involved in the events following Pelham's death and leading to the Pitt–Newcastle ministry, in which he made the most of the lucrative opportunities

143

afforded by the office of Paymaster-General. He felt that Shelburne and George III had both conspired against his ambition of an earldom and his son, Charles James, perpetuated the family feud.

Franklin: Benjamin (1706–90) Scientist, inventor, writer, politician and diplomat, he helped draft and subsequently signed the Declaration of Independence. Although born in Boston he established his reputation in Pennsylvania, leading radical opposition to proprietorial interests. Was the chief author of the Albany plan for union in 1754. Acted on behalf of Pennsylvania in London from 1757 and was agent for Pennsylvania, Georgia and Massachusetts. Helped secure the repeal of the Stamp Act but was greatly censured in England for his part in the Hutchinson Letters affair. Returned to Pennsylvania in 1775, was a member of the second Continental Congress and was sent to Versailles as one of three to negotiate a treaty with France in 1776. Played a major part in the peace negotiations of 1781–3.

Gage: Thomas (1719–87) Commended for his courage and resourcefulness at the defeat of Braddock in 1755, he stayed in America and was Governor of Montreal (1760–63), becoming Amherst's successor as Commander-in-Chief in 1763. He concentrated his troops increasingly in the east as political troubles increased. Left America in 1773 but was sent back in 1774 as Commander and also Governor of Massachusetts. Was felt to be insufficiently vigorous and was reinforced by other generals, Howe succeeding him officially as Commander-in-Chief in 1776 though, unofficially, a year earlier.

Germain: (Sackville) Lord George (1716–85) Born Sackville, the third son of the Earl of Dorset, he acquired the name Germain to inherit a fortune. MP for various constituencies (1741–82), he was also a career soldier with a reputation as a brave and competent officer, becoming Commander of the British forces in Germany in 1758 despite George II's opposition. But his odd behaviour at Minden in preventing a total victory by failing to advance his cavalry led to court martial and ignominy. It is thought that jealousy of Brunswick was the cause of his action. With the new reign his political fortunes revived. A brief flirtation with the Rockinghamites and a period of independence did not prevent his being made Secretary of State for America (1775–82). His chief failings here were in placing too much reliance on Loyalists and in quarrelling with most of his colleagues, both military and civilian.

Grafton: Augustus Henry Fitzroy (1735–1811) third Duke of His political career began in opposition to Bute and he became Secretary of State for the North under Rockingham at the age of 30, resigning on the failure of the First Lord to secure the services of Pitt. A reluctant First Lord in Chatham's administration and subsequently he suffered from lack of authority while Pitt was ill. Strengthened by Pitt's retirement and by the acquisition of Bedford and North his last two years were bedevilled by Wilkes and Junius. Resigned in 1770 but served North outside the cabinet, as Lord Privy Seal (1771–5). Unhappy with the direction of American policy he resigned. He last held office as Lord Privy Seal in Rockingham's administration (1782–83).

Grenville: George (1712–70) MP for Buckingham (1741–70), his early career was overshadowed by his overbearing brother Richard, Lord Temple, and William Pitt, from 1754 Grenville's brother-in-law. In 1754, '56 and '57 he was passed over for preferment but entered the new reign in favour with Bute and the Court. He refused Pitt's office in 1761, fearing Pitt and not trusting his colleagues Newcastle and Fox. By 1762 the office of Chancellor of the Exchequer was beneath him and he refused it from Bute, to whom he no longer wished to play second fiddle. Secretary of State briefly in 1762 and First Lord of the Admiralty in 1763 before his elevation to the Treasury.

Halifax: George Montagu Dunk (1716–71) second Earl of A holder of minor court, legal and military office before being made President of the Board of Trade in 1748. A vigorous head of his department, he pushed British colonial, especially American, trading interests. Halifax, capital of his new colony of Nova Scotia, is named after him. But his efforts to put all colonial trade and business under his aegis and develop a third secretaryship of the colonies failed, with possibly serious consequences for British control in America. He resigned in 1756 but held the office again (1757–61). He was Secretary of State for the North (1762) and South (1763) and was one of the issuers of the famous General Warrant against those concerned with Number 45 of the *North Briton*. Left office with Grenville in 1765.

Hancock: John (1737–93) A businessman millionaire of Boston whose trading activities, like his vessels, sailed close to the wind and aroused the ire of customs officers. In 1768 his sloop *Liberty* was seized by Boston customs officials and the subsequent riots caused the officials to flee to Castle William and the government to send troops to Boston. A close ally of Sam Adams, his cash was an asset to agitation. President of the Massachusetts Provincial Congress, member of the Continental Congress (1775–80) and the first Governor of Massachusetts (1780).

Henry: Patrick (1736–99) Son of a Scottish immigrant, he became a lawyer and, in 1765, a member of the Virginia House of Burgesses, championing the cause of the underprivileged frontier and backwater against the eastern oligarchy. Responsible for the Virginia Resolves against the Stamp Act, becoming a leading figure in Virginian politics, delegate to the first Continental Congress and leading organiser of military resistance in Virginia. Governor of Virginia (1776–79 and 1784–86).

Hillsborough: Hill Wills (1718–97) first Earl of Became a member of the House of Lords, after a career in the Irish Parliament, in 1746. President of the Board of Trade (1763–65) and Secretary of State for America (1768–72). He was firm on the need to preserve and defend Parliament's rights in the colonies and was responsible for ordering troops into Boston in 1768, against Hutchinson's advice. He continued to urge a policy of firmness as Secretary of State for the North (1779–82).

Howe: Richard (1726–99) Admiral Elder brother of William. MP for Dartmouth (1757–82). He was given naval command in America in 1776 and joined his brother who had been acting as army commander since 1776. He insisted that the two brothers be allowed authority also as peace commissioners. Shared in the New York campaign in 1776 and the fruitless peace negotiations of the same period. Resigned in 1778.

Howe: William (1727–1814) General A friend of Wolfe, he had a very distinguished career in the Seven Years' War at Quebec, Montreal and Havana and was a popular officer. MP for Nottingham (1756–86) but did not speak before 1770. Unhappy about the breach with the colonists but did not refuse the succession to Gage in 1776, having been in America since 1775. Never considered that he was sufficiently supplied with troops to defeat the colonists and was happy to act as a conciliator. His unhappiness increased with the Declaration of Independence and explains his refusal to risk his army in a decisive battle against Washington in the New York campaign of 1776 and the fruitless peace negotiations accompanying it. His relations with Germain, initially good, deteriorated from 1777 and in 1778 he was succeeded by Clinton.

Hutchinson: Thomas (1711–80) A leading Massachusetts conservative, he was Lieutenant-Governor from 1758 and Chief Justice in 1760, thus arousing the anger of James Otis's father who coveted the post. He opposed Grenville's measures on economic rather than political grounds, but his brother-in-law was Stamp Collector, and Hutchinson sought to enforce the measures. His house was sacked by a mob in August 1765. Acting as Governor from 1765, he succeeded to the post from 1771–74. His unpopularity was sealed by the Hutchinson letters affair, when letters to English friends, arguing for stronger measures against the colonists, fell into Franklin's hands. He left Massachusetts in 1774, never able to return.

Jebb: John (1736–86) An Anglican clergyman with strong Unitarian views, supporting the Feather's Tavern petition of 1772 which sought to relieve clergy from the need to subscribe to the Thirty-Nine Articles. He resigned his benefice, took up medicine, and became involved in the radical politics of London and Westminster. He was a close associate of Cartwright in the campaign for radical parliamentary reform.

Jefferson: Thomas (1743–1826) One of the 'Founding Fathers' of the United States and chief author of the Declaration of Independence, he was the third President of the United States, a scientist and an architect as well as owner of a slave plantation. Of old Virginian stock, he practised at the bar, entered the House of Burgesses in 1769 and was elected to the Continental Congress in 1775. His *Summary View of the Rights of America* in 1774 placed him high among the radical opponents of British pretensions. As Governor of Virginia (1799–81), he proved himself an incompetent leader against British invasion.

Jenkinson: Charles (1729–1808) first Earl of Liverpool MP for various constituencies (1761–89), a Whig of an old Tory background who saw himself as a government rather than a party man. At first private secretary to Bute and then one of the secretaries to the Treasury under Grenville, he succeeded in remaining on good terms with both. He adhered to every ministry from Pitt's in 1766 to North's in 1782 and again to the Younger Pitt from 1784. He was seen to be a very influential figure in North's war administration. As Secretary at War (1778–82), he had direct access to the King who consulted him on appointments and cabinet politics. Refused all higher office, preferring the role of bureaucrat and *eminence grise*. Continued to advise the King during the awkward years of 1782–84.

Keppel: Hon. Augustus (1725–86) Admiral MP (1755–82). Cousin to the third Duke of Richmond. One of the officers on Byng's court martial in 1757, he tried to secure a reprieve. In the Seven Years' War he saw distinguished service and after the war gravitated politically towards Cumberland and Rockingham, and was a Lord of the Admiralty (1765–66). A bitter opponent of the war against the colonists, he refused command in American waters but was given command of the Channel fleet in 1776, despite his political unsuitability and his lowly position among the Admirals. He was on good terms with Sandwich but in June 1778 forbore to meet a superior French fleet and in July failed to prevent its escape off Ushant. A subsequent controversy with a subordinate, Admiral Palliser, was extremely bitter and he became entangled in Westminster politics, which created a breach with Sandwich. His acquittal in a court martial led to celebratory riots and demands for Sandwich's dismissal, though the latter had acted honourably throughout. The incident underlies how political wrangles undermined unity in the fight against the colonists and their allies.

Newcastle: Thomas Pelham-Holles (1673–1768) Duke of Duke of both Newcastle-upon-Tyne and Under-Lyme, he inherited vast wealth which he largely dissipated on political expenditure. Lord Chamberlain (1717–24); Secretary of State for the South (1724–48); Secretary of State for the North (1748–54); First Lord of the Treasury (1754–56, 1757–62); Lord Privy Seal (1765–66). A much ridiculed statesman, he was in fact a shrewd, knowledgeable and industrious servant of the Crown and the Whigs, despite his foibles and weaknesses.

North: Frederick (1732–92) Lord MP for Banbury (1754–90), son of the first Earl of Guilford. A Lord of the Treasury (1759–65); Paymaster-General (1766–67); Chancellor of the Exchequer (1767–82); First Lord of the Treasury (1770–82); Home Secretary (1783).

Otis: James (1725–83) Of old Massachusetts stock, the son of Colonel James Otis, James Otis followed his father into the law and pursued the family quarrel against Hutchinson. He resigned as the King's Advocate General, refusing to accept the legality of Writs of Assistance raising the cry, 'taxation without representation is tyranny'. He entered the House of Representatives in 1761, headed the Massachusetts Committee of Correspondence in 1764 and presided over the re-creation of the non-importation agreements in 1767. Virulent in speech, he nonetheless acted as a brake on the more physical tactics of Sam Adams and others. A brawl in 1769 left him mentally unstable and he took no further part in radical activities.

Pelham: Hon. Henry (1696–1754) MP for Seaford (1717–22); Sussex (1722–54). He was the younger brother of the Duke of Newcastle but not the junior partner. A Lord of the Treasury (1721–24); Secretary at War (1724–30); Paymaster-General (1730–43); First Lord of the Treasury and Chancellor of the Exchequer (1743–54).

Pitt: William (the Elder, 1708–78) first Earl of Chatham After 1754 brother-in-law of the second Earl Temple and George Grenville. Joint Vice-Treasurer for Ireland (1746); Paymaster-General (1746–55); Secretary of State for the South (1756–57, 1757–61); Lord Privy Seal (1766–68). Despite the reputation he won in the Seven Years' War, he held high office rarely. He was not able to square his passion for dictatorial independence with the aristocratic and patronage politics of the time. At times his oratory was effective but he could not rid himself of empty histrionics which limited his effectiveness.

Pitt: William (the Younger, 1759–1805) MP for Appleby (1781–84), Cambridge University (1784–1806). The second son of Chatham, he was hampered in his career by lack of money. A supporter and ally of Christopher Wyvill in the Association Movement, he supported parliamentary reform in his early years, and made his maiden speech in support of Burke's economic reforms. He quickly gained the respect of the House, refused office in 1782 because of his dislike of party, but was Chancellor of the Exchequer at the age of 24 in Shelburne's ministry. He made it impossible for Shelburne to agree terms with North for a coalition. He declined the highest office on Shelburne's fall but accepted it in 1783 to save the Crown from control by party.

Portland: William Bentinck (1738–1809) third Duke of On succeeding to the title in 1762 he attached himself to Rockingham and was Lord Chamberlain 1765–66. He opposed Grafton (1768–70) with more than political hostility. Lord Lieutenant of Ireland in 1782, he left office with Fox and was First Lord of the Treasury in the Fox–North coalition of 1783.

Price: Dr Richard (1723–91) Of dissenter background and education, he was a philosopher, mathematician and, in matters of religion, a Unitarian. He numbered among his friends Hume, Franklin and Shelburne, and his writings on financial matters influenced Pitt's reforms after 1784. Wrote pamphlets attacking the war and was made a freeman of the City of London. In 1789 his sermon praising the French Revolution provoked Burke to write his *Reflections*.

Priestley: Joseph (1733–1804) A teacher, theologian and scientist of international repute, he was a dissenting minister. Librarian to Shelburne at Bowood (1772–80), where he carried out some of his most famous experiments. He then lived at Birmingham where he was the victim of the riots of 1791. With Franklin, he co-wrote pamphlets supporting the American cause and was a protagonist of parliamentary reform.

Richmond: Charles Lennox (1735–1806) third Duke of Entered the Lords in 1756, quarrelled with the new King in 1760 and associated himself with Rockingham and Newcastle. His appointment as Secretary of State in succession to Grafton in 1766 was seen as particularly insulting to George III. Despite his grandee status he was a supporter of parliamentary reform, advocating in 1776 annual Parliaments, manhood suffrage and equal electoral districts, though not the ungentlemanly ballot. He moved for conciliation with the colonists in 1770 and argued in the Lords in 1775 that their actions were 'perfectly justifiable'. Master of the Ordnance (1782), he did not resign with his nephew Fox in 1782 but quit Shelburne's ministry in April 1783. He took the same office under Pitt in December 1783.

Rigby: Richard (1722–88) MP for various constituencies (1745–88) as a protégé of the Duke of Bedford. Joint Paymaster-General (1768–82), he had previously secured minor offices with the Duke's patronage in 1755, 1757 and 1762. On Bedford's death in 1771, he continued to pursue policies towards America which the Bedfordites had adopted and justified the war to the bitter end.

Rockingham: Charles Watson-Wentworth (1730–82) Marquess of A wealthy Yorkshire landowner who before 1760 held no national political office and who was a notably inept speaker in the Lords. His influence came through his character and his wealth, enabling him to succeed the ageing and bankrupt Newcastle as leader of the opposition Whigs. He became First Lord of the Treasury twice, in 1765–66 and again in 1782.

Rodney: George Brydges (1719–92) Admiral Service in the Seven Years' War secured him the position of Commander-in-Chief on the Leeward Islands towards the end of the war, and he was able to snap up French and Spanish possessions. He was an MP (1751–74 and 1780–82), but a cripplingly expensive electoral contest at Northampton in 1768 encouraged him to return to sea in 1771 in the hope of reviving his fortunes. Unfortunately, he was less successful than he hoped and he quarrelled with the ministry over its refusal to allow him to remain Governor of Greenwich Hospital, to award him the Governorship of Jamaica, or to pay money greatly overdue to him. Returning to England in 1774 he was forced to flee to France to escape creditors and in 1778 he could return to Britain only with the assistance of a loan from Marshal Biron. At last, in 1779, he was made Commander-in-Chief of the Leeward Islands and on his way captured a Spanish convoy and relieved Gibraltar, for which he received a pension. His time in the West Indies was unhappy. He made himself unpopular with the merchants and other residents of the captured island of St Eustatius, fell ill and had an uneasy relationship with Admiral Hood, who was his second-in-command and who succeeded him when Rodney went home in 1789. In England the Rockingham opposition accused him of plundering the island of St Eustatius for his own profit. He returned to the West Indies in 1782 but even his victory at Les Saintes in 1782 was not without controversy as he was accused of failing to follow up the victory. Even before news of his success reached London the Rockingham ministry had decided to recall him.

Sandwich: John Montagu (171–92) fourth Earl of Attached to the Duke of Bedford's interest from the time of his entry into politics in 1739, he was a member of the Admiralty Board during much of the War of Austrian Succession, playing a leading part in its affairs. Subsequently he played a major role in the peace negotiations with France in 1747–48 and was rewarded with the position of First Lord of the Admiralty which he held, working closely with Admiral Anson, until 1751. He notoriously took part in the prosecution of Wilkes in 1763. Postmaster-General (1768–70); Secretary of State for the North (1770–71); First Lord of the Admiralty (1771–82).

Sawbridge: John (1732–95) MP for Hythe (1768–74) and London (1774–80 1780–95). A landowner, distiller and Alderman of the City of London, he opposed the ministry over the Middlesex election and was a founder member of the Society of Supporters of the Bill of Rights. He broke with Wilkes in 1773 and opposed Wilkes's candidacy as Lord Mayor, but was reconciled with him in 1774 and helped formulate a common City programme for shorter Parliaments, place bills, electoral reform and support for America. Every year from 1771 he introduced a motion into the Commons for shorter Parliaments but fell victim to the law of diminishing returns.

Shelburne: William Fitzmaurice Petty (1737–1805) second Earl of (later Marquess of Lansdowne) Entered the House of Lords at Westminster in 1765, initially as a protégé of Bute, but quickly developed an independent stance, transferring his allegiance to Pitt in 1763 after a brief period as President of the Board of Trade. As Secretary of State for the South (1766–68), he sought conciliation and the raising of a colonial revenue without recourse to parliamentary taxation. Although estranged from his colleagues, he did not resign until Chatham led the way in 1768, despite Hillsborough becoming Secretary of State for America. He opposed General Warrants and Wilkes's expulsion in 1768, and helped organise the petitioning campaign of 1769–70. He succeeded Chatham as leader of the Chathamites in 1778 and Rockingham as First Lord in 1782. He was patron of the City radical movements and of such enlightenment figures as Dr Price, Joseph Priestley and Jeremy Bentham. His friends included Benjamin Franklin, the Comte de Mirabeau and Samuel Romilly, but in political life he fatally failed to secure the trust of colleagues.

Temple: Richard Grenville (1711–79) second Earl MP (1734–57). Inherited large estates and was a significant but destructive political figure: as First Lord of the Admiralty in the Pitt–

Devonshire ministry (1756–57), he showed incompetence in administration and, despite Pitt's support, was not returned to the office in the Pitt–Newcastle ministry, where he was Lord Privy Seal until resigning with Pitt in 1761. He was patron to the *North Briton* and John Wilkes. Instrumental in preventing the formation of a Pitt ministry in 1765, he refused the Treasury in 1766 and quarrelled with Pitt.

Thurlow: Edward (1731–1806) first Baron MP for Tamworth (1765–78); Solicitor General (1770–71); Attorney-General (1771–78); Lord Chancellor from 1778 to April 1783 and December 1783 to 1792. Brought into the Bedford group through his friendship with Lord Weymouth, he was a keen supporter of a strong line against the colonists, voting against Stamp Act repeal and remaining in North's administration until the end. He was used by George III in political negotiations from 1778 and especially between 1782 and 1784.

Townsend: James (1737–87) MP for West Looe (1767–74), Calne (1782–87); Lord Mayor of London (1772–73). Brought into Parliament by Shelburne and an immediate advocate of Wilkes's cause, he was not a great success as a parliamentarian but was an effective leader of Shelburne's City of London interest. He broke with Wilkes in 1771 and formed the Constitutional Society with John Horne.

Townshend: Hon. Charles (1725–67) Sat for various constituencies in the family interest from 1746 to 1767. Secretary at War (1761–62); First Lord of Trade (1763); Paymaster-General (1765–67); Chancellor of the Exchequer (1766–67). Described by Sir Lewis Namier thus: 'Admired but not esteemed, trusted and believed by no one, he astonished and amused, which satisfied his vanity.' A fine speaker, his political career was consistent only in its inconsistency, but he did pursue a steady policy on America, urging his great-uncle Newcastle in 1754 to give up the idea of a union for colonial defence, and to strengthen controls over the colonies and to establish parliamentary taxation in America.

Trecothick: Barlow (1718–75) MP for London (1768–74); Lord Mayor of London (June–November 1770); colonial agent for New Hampshire (1766–74). Spent much of his youth in Boston, Massachusetts, where it is possible that he was born. Was involved in North American trade and was also a West Indies plantation owner. His closest political association was with Rockingham and he was the leading figure outside Parliament organising the campaign for the repeal of the Stamp Act. Was a link between Rockingham and the City but he was hostile to Wilkes, which limited his effectiveness. Was an increasingly sympathetic friend to the American colonists.

Wedderburn: Alexander (1733–1805) first Baron Loughborough MP (1761–69; 1770–80). Of Scottish birth and legal training, he was called to the English Bar and entered Parliament in Bute's interest, continuing to support the administration of Grenville but going into opposition in 1765. He voted against the repeal of the Stamp Act and for Wilkes's expulsion in 1768, despite Grenville's opposition to it. Turned out of his seat for opposing Grafton's administration in 1769, he was returned in 1770 and entered into the North ministry with Grenville's followers in 1771. Gave wholehearted support to Parliament's cause in America but was increasingly vexed by North's leadership. His insistence on becoming a peer and chief justice of common pleas created a ministerial crisis (1778–79), but he was successful in both aims in 1780.

Whately: Thomas (1728–72) MP (1761–72) Secretary to the Treasury (1763–65); A Lord of Trade (1771); Under-Secretary of State for the North (1771–72). Bute secured Whately his first seat in Parliament. Grenville's private secretary for brief periods in 1762 and 1765, and was in Grenville's connection until the latter's death. Chief architect of the Stamp Act. From 1768 Whately was strategist and chief whip of the connection, especially during the Wilkes crisis of 1769–70.

Wilkes: John (1725–87) MP for Aylesbury (1757–64); Middlesex (1769–69; 1774–90); Lord Mayor of London (1774–75). '. . . his character infamous, his life stained with every vice' but, Edward Gibbon also wrote, 'he has inexhaustible spirits, infinite wit and a great deal of humour.' Always in severe financial difficulties, he had reason to regret the resignation of his patrons, Temple and Pitt, in 1761. He turned to journalism with consequences which are famous. Expelled from the House of Commons in 1764 and forced to retreat to France, he returned in 1768, provoking the events that followed his election for Middlesex. Disliked by the politicians for his vices, his independence and his popularity with such a large proportion of the population, he was admired by the 'middling and inferior set' for his independence, as a symbol of resistance to authority and as a fellow sufferer at the hands of an aristocratic social and political system. He adopted, late, parliamentary reform, but his radicalism was much abated by 1780 when his actions against the Gordon rioters lost him much popular support. He was a strong supporter of Pitt the Younger in 1784.

Wyvill: Reverend Christopher (1740–1822), An Anglican clergyman who inherited a large family estate on marrying his cousin, he was unable to enter Parliament but used his political skills in extra-parliamentary agitation, becoming secretary, later chairman, of the Yorkshire Association and largely directing the Association Movement. He believed that the American war and high taxes were being protracted to suit the interests of the Crown and its servants, maintained by a corrupt House of Commons, elected through closed boroughs. He therefore sought parliamentary as well as economic reform to make the House of Commons more independent, especially by replacing pocket boroughs with open constituencies in the counties and larger boroughs. Unfortunately, his Movement was ground between the conservative allies he needed in Parliament and the extreme radicals of the Westminster Association. The end of the war in 1782 and, earlier, the Gordon Riots, as well as the conservatism of the gentry, reduced the Movement's effectiveness very quickly.

Appendix II: A Brief Chronology of Events 1754–84

Britain			America
Duke of Newcastle becomes First Lord of the Treasury	1754	March	
		June–July	Albany Convention
		July	Washington's defeat by the French
	1755	July	Defeat of Braddock
Dismissal of William Pitt		November	
Britain declares war on France Loss of Minorca	1756	May	
Duke of Newcastle resigns		October	
Pitt–Newcastle ministry formed	1757	June	
	1758	July	Capture of Louisburg from France
	1759	July	Capture of Fort Ticonderoga
		September	Capture of Quebec
	1760	September	Capture of Montreal
Accession of George III		October	
	1761	February	The Writs of Assistance Case
Resignation of Pitt		October	
Resignation of Newcastle; Bute is made First Lord of the Treasury	1762	May	
Peace of Paris	1763	February	
George Grenville replaces Bute Wilkes and the 'No. 45'		April	

Britain		America
1763		
	May	Pontiac's rebellion
Proclamation Act	October	
1764		
Sugar Act	March	
Currency Act		
1765		
Stamp Act	March	
Quartering Act	April/May	
Regency Crisis		
	May	Virginia Resolves
Rockingham Ministry	July	
	August	Riots in Boston, etc.
	October	Stamp Act Congress meets
1766		
Repeal of Stamp Act	March	
Declaratory Act		
Duke of Grafton resigns	April	Radicals secure control of House of Representatives in Massachusetts
Chatham ministry formed	July	
1767		
Townshend's promise to raise a revenue in America and cut land tax	February	
Townshend's Revenue Act	May	
	October	Beginning of non-importation movement (1767–70)
	December	The first of Dickinson's *Farmer's Letters* published

Year	Month		
1768	February	Massachusetts Assembly's first Circular Letter	Wilkes elected for Middlesex
	March	St George's Fields 'Massacre'	
	May	The 'Liberty' affair	
	October	Redcoats arrive in Boston	Chatham's resignation
1769	February	Wilkes expelled from House of Commons	Society of the Supporters of the Bill of Rights formed
	April		Luttrell chosen as MP for Middlesex
1770	February		Lord North becomes First Lord of the Treasury
	March	Boston Massacre	Partial repeal of Townshend duties
1771	July	Last non-importation agreement abandoned	
1772	June	*Gaspée* incident	
	December	Boston Committee of Correspondence established	
1773	May	Hutchinson Letters affair	Tea Act
	June		East India Company Regulatory Act
	December	Boston Tea Party	
1774	March to June		'The Intolerable Acts' passed
	September	First Continental Congress meets	Quebec Act
	October	The Continental Association adopted	General Election

159

Britain			America
	1775	January	Howe, Clinton, Burgoyne sent to America
Chatham's conciliation proposals		February	
North's conciliation proposals			
New England Trade and Fisheries Act			
		April	Lexington and Concord
Burke's first conciliation proposals		May	Rebel seizure of forts at Crown Point and Ticonderoga
		June	Second Continental Congress
			Creation of Continental Army
			Bunker Hill
		July	Olive Branch Petition adopted
			Invasion of Canada
Burke's second conciliation proposals		November	
	1776	January	Tom Paine's *Common Sense* published
Wilkes presents his parliamentary reform proposals		March	British evacuation of Boston
		July	Declaration of Independence
		June–Oct	New York Campaign
		September	Staten Island Peace Conference
	1777	September	Howe takes Philadelphia
		October	Surrender of Burgoyne at Saratoga
Irish crisis begins. Volunteer Associations formed (1778–9)	1778	February	France allies with America

160

North attempts to secure Chatham's services	March	Earl of Carlisle Peace Commission in America
	April–June	Clinton succeeds Howe as Commander-in-Chief.
	May	British withdrawal from Philadelphia
Keppel's inability to bring French fleet to decisive action	July	
	December	British military activity in South. Georgia taken.
Keppel's acquittal	1779 February	
Spain declares war on Britain	June	
	July	French fleet off America
Attempted invasion of Britain by Franco-Spanish fleet	August	
Resignation from the government of Lord Gower	October	
Resignation from the government of Viscount Weymouth	November	
Beginnings of Wyvill's Association Movement	December	
Admiral Rodney lifts Spanish siege of Gibraltar	1780 January	
The Yorkshire Petition presented	February	
Burke's scheme for economical reform presented to House of Commons	March	
Dunning's resolutions.		
Foundation of Society for Constitutional Information	April	

Britain		America
The Gordon Riots	May	Charleston surrenders to Clinton
	June	French army in New England
	July	British victory over Americans at Camden
	August	
Britain declares war on Holland	December	
	1781 February	Rodney takes St Eustatius
	March	British victory at Guilford Court House
September	October	Naval battle at Chesapeake Bay
News of Yorktown reaches Britain	November	Yorktown surrenders
Spain takes Minorca	1782 February	
Rockingham Ministry formed	March	
Crewe's Act, Clerke's Act and Burke's Establishment Act passed	April	Battle of Les Saintes
Independent Irish Parliament created	April–May	
Death of Rockingham. Shelburne becomes First Lord. Fox resigns.	May	
	July	
Peace preliminaries signed at Versailles	November	

Event	Year	Month	
Defeat of peace preliminaries in House of Commons	1783	February	
Fox–North coalition formed		April	
Definitive peace proposals at Versailles		September	
		November	British evacuation of New York
Pitt becomes First Lord of the Treasury		December	
General Election	1784	March	

APPENDIX III: THE CHIEF ADMINISTRATIONS, 1754–84: A SUMMARY

Newcastle	March 1754 – October 1756
Pitt–Devonshire	November 1756 – April 1757
Pitt–Newcastle	June 1757 – October 1761
Newcastle–Bute	October 1761 – May 1762
Bute	May 1762 – April 1763
Grenville	April 1763 – July 1765
Rockingham	July 1765 – August 1766
Grafton–Pitt	August 1766 – October 1768
Grafton	to January 1770
North	February 1770 – March 1782
Rockingham	March 1782 – June 1782
Shelburne	July 1782 – April 1783
Fox–North Coalition	April 1783 – December 1783
William Pitt	December 1783 – February 1801

APPENDIX IV: CHIEF OFFICE HOLDERS, 1754–84

First Lord of the Treasury

March 1754	The Duke of Newcastle
October 1756	The Duke of Devonshire
June 1757	The Duke of Newcastle
May 1762	Earl of Bute
April 1763	Marquis of Rockingham
August 1766	Duke of Grafton
February 1770	Lord North
March 1782	Marquis of Rockingham
July 1782	Earl of Shelburne
April 1783	Duke of Portland
December 1783	William Pitt

Lord President of the Council

June 1751	Earl Granville
September 1763	Duke of Bedford
July 1765	Earl of Winchelsea
July 1766	Earl of Northington
December 1767	Earl Gower
November 1779	Earl Bathurst
March 1782	Lord Camden
April 1783	Viscount Stormont
December 1783	Earl Gower

Secretary of State for the North

March 1754	Earl of Holdernesse
March 1761	Earl of Bute

March 1762	George Grenville
October 1762	Earl of Halifax
September 1763	Earl of Sandwich
July 1765	Duke of Grafton
May 1766	General Conway
January 1768	Viscount Weymouth
October 1768	Earl of Rochford
December 1770	Earl of Sandwich
January 1771	Earl of Halifax
June 1771	Earl of Suffolk
October 1779–1782	Viscount Stormont

Office abolished

Secretary of State for the South

March 1754	Sir Thomas Robinson
November 1755	Henry Fox
October 1756	William Pitt
October 1761	Earl of Egremont
September 1763	Earl of Halifax
July 1765	General Conway
May 1766	Duke of Richmond
August 1766	Earl of Shelburne
October 1768	Viscount Weymouth
December 1770	Earl of Rochford
November 1775	Viscount Weymouth
November 1779– March 1782	Earl of Hillsborough

Office abolished

Secretary of State for the American Colonies

January 1768	Earl of Hillsborough
August 1772	Earl of Dartmouth
November 1779– February 1782	Lord George Germain
February 1782	Welbore Ellis

Office abolished

Secretary of State for Home (and Colonial) Affairs

March 1782	Earl of Shelburne
July 1782	Thomas Townshend
April 1783	Lord North

December 19–23 1783	Earl Temple
December 23 1783	Lord Sydney (Thomas Townshend)

Secretary of State for Foreign Affairs

March 1782	Charles James Fox
July 1782	Lord Grantham
April 1783	Charles James Fox
December 19–23 1783	Earl Temple
December 23 1783	Marquis of Carmarthen

President of the Board of Trade

October 1748	Earl of Halifax
March 1761	Lord Sandys
March 1763	Charles Townshend
April 1763	Earl of Shelburne
September 1763	Earl of Hillsborough
July 1765	Earl of Dartmouth
August 1766	Earl of Hillsborough
December 1766	Robert Nugent
January 1768	Earl of Hillsborough
August 1772	Earl of Dartmouth
November 1775	Lord George Germain
September 1780	Earl of Carlisle
December 1780	Lord Grantham

June 1782 office temporarily suppressed

Lord Chancellor

February 1737	Earl of Hardwicke
June 1757	Robert Henley
(Keeper of the Great Seal)	
January 1761	Baron Henley, later Earl of Northington (1764)
July 1766	Lord Camden
January 17 1770	Charles Yorke
January 20 1770	In Commission
January 23 1771	Lord Apsley (Earl Bathurst 1771)
June 1778	Lord Thurlow

Chancellor of the Exchequer

April 1754	Henry Legge
November 1755	Sir George Lyttelton

November 1756	Henry Legge
April 1757	(office vacant)
July 1757	Henry Legge
March 1761	Viscount Barrington
May 1761	Sir Frances Dashwood
April 1763	George Grenville
July 1765	William Dowdeswell
September 1767	Lord Mansfield
December 1770	Lord North
March 1782	Lord John Cavendish
July 1782	William Pitt
April 1783	Lord John Cavendish
December 1783	William Pitt

Secretary at War

May 1746	Henry Fox
October 1755	Viscount Barrington
March 1761	Charles Townshend
December 1762	Welbore Ellis
July 1765	Viscount Barrington
December 1778	Charles Jenkinson
March 1782	Thomas Townshend
July 1782	Sir George Yonge
April 1783	Richard Fitzpatrick
December 1783	Sir George Yonge

First Lord of the Admiralty

June 1751	Lord Anson
November 1756	Earl Temple
April 1757	(office vacant)
April 1757	Lord Anson
June 1762	Earl of Halifax
January 1763	George Grenville
April 1763	Earl of Sandwich
September 1763	Earl of Egmont
September 1766	Sir Charles Saunders
December 1766	Sir Edward Hawke
January 1771	Earl of Sandwich
March 1782	Viscount Keppel
December 1783	Viscount Howe

INDEX

Index